Oppositional Defiant Disorder 101

The Ultimate in-Depth Guide For Parents to Understand Oppositional Defiant Disorder in Children and Teenagers

Kathleen D. McIntosh

contained within this document, including, but not limited to, errors, omissions, or inaccuracies.

Table of Contents

Introduction

Every parent's journey is simultaneously similar and unique. There are things all parents experience—the anxiety of whether their baby is going to be born healthy, the joy when their little one says its first words or gives its first steps, shedding a tear when they go to preschool, and wondering why it feels like you're in a time warp because they grow up so fast. These are things all parents can relate to and talk about often; your parents will often tell you how time flies, and you only realize it once you have children of your own. What makes each parent's journey unique is who they are as a person and who their children are. How healthy their children are. Whether parents are still together or separated. I had the experience of raising my child on my own, and I initially worked and then attended college as well. Keeping an eye on her development was difficult because I wasn't always there. It hit me one day that she was acting in a way that was upsetting; her demeanor wasn't that of an upset child but more of a proverbial possessed child. Her refusal to get off the floor in the grocery store, screaming, and throwing her shoes left me speechless. I felt an incredible sensation of guilt come over me and I thought that it must be because she spends so much time at my mom's and I only see her from late in the afternoon. When I tried to pick her up, she started hitting me, and I just ran out of the store and drove home.

She has always been opinionated and extroverted, but, looking back, that was the first sign of Oppositional Defiant Disorder I can clearly distinguish from other difficult behavior. At that point, I thought that maybe she wasn't feeling well, and maybe she had a fever, but she wouldn't allow me to take her temperature. I started to get angry, and this just blew up the situation. I closed her in her room and she spent more than half an hour banging on the door before there was silence. When I went into her room a few minutes after things died down, she had fallen asleep on the floor, so I put her to bed. For a day or two, nothing happened except for a protest against some peas on her plate.

Then she flared up again, this time at school. I was between classes when I received a call from her school's principal, asking me to come to pick her up. A boy on the playground told her she had ugly big toes, so she apparently went into a screaming fit and threw sand in his eyes. The principal told me that her behavior has taken a turn for the worse, and advised me to get her checked out by a doctor or a psychologist. That's where my journey started and also where my inspiration came from to find out everything I possibly can about Oppositional Defiant Disorder, a tragic psychiatric condition that not only affects the well-being of your child, but also you as a parent, and the siblings.

Oppositional Defiant Disorder 101 is exactly that: it contains all the basics you need to know about children and teenagers who have this psychiatric disorder, but it is also so much more. Your guide starts with explaining and describing your child's behavior, what the possible causes of the behavior are, it includes statistical information you may want to know about regarding this disorder, and, most importantly, it also gives you crucial information about other disorders that can commonly co-occur with Oppositional Defiant Disorder. The guide provides information based on the most recent research and because there are so many angles from which one can approach this disorder, making this guide a watertight one was non-negotiable.

An interesting component added to the guide is a discussion of how a child's ability to understand and manage emotions develop within their brain, and how hormones affect a teenager's ability to make decisions and process emotions. The guide is focused on your health as a parent, the health of your child with Oppositional Defiant Disorder, and also the health of siblings if you have more than one child.

Another segment based on recent and relevant strategies in the guide you'd want to look into is how to get the most out of disciplining your child by doing it productively. Learn how to use tools like positive reinforcement, understand the crucial underpinning factor that is consistent, and empower the siblings to understand the situation and deal with it effectively. A chapter in this guide that I hope you will find rewarding is the chapter on family that includes family activities, family goals, and how to stay close and appreciate each other. And, stay strong by sticking to the three P's—you'll see what they are once you've immersed yourself into the guide.

Is there anything special your child needs to eat if they are struggling with Oppositional Defiant Disorder? You can learn more about the benefits of certain nutrients and the importance of focusing on health. If you are a follower of holistic medicine, you may find some information you need about remedies of this nature. Finally, remember to read about how to look after yourself, your relationship, and why this is crucial for your child's health.

Are you ready for positive change? This guide arms you with the first two steps towards conquering Oppositional Defiant Disorder and creating a healthier environment for your child. These steps involve knowledge and understanding. You can achieve what you want for your family if you use these rocks to build on. As parents, we want the best for our children, and it hurts us deeply to see them suffering. In a situation where your child or teenager has Oppositional Defiant Disorder, it can feel like your hands are tied, and your child's behavior toward you and the rest of your family can cause deep wounds. It's time to empower yourself through understanding and by using knowledge and tried-and-tested techniques to become the strong parent you are meant to be. May you find your inspiration in this guide, and may it enforce love and respect between you, your family, and your ODD child.

Chapter 1:

ODD: What All Parents Need To

Know

At first, you may think your child's rebellious behavior is normal when they are still young; after all, toddlers are notorious for behaving in demanding and challenging ways. However, as they get older, and this kind of behavior doesn't become less frequent, what are your first thoughts supposed to be? All children and teenagers exhibit acts of defiance, a disregard for rules and authority figures, and vindictiveness from time to time. More typically, children are prone to throw tantrums while teenagers tend to be snotty, irritable, and extremely moody. When this behavior becomes applicable to Oppositional Defiant Disorder, children and teens' behavior suddenly becomes excessive and destructive and is most likely causing havoc in the child's personal life or at school.

Before defining Oppositional Defiant Disorder, it is important to distinguish between Oppositional Defiant behavior, which is a behavior present in all teenagers and children, and when it starts to manifest as Oppositional Defiant Disorder or ODD. Oppositional Defiant Disorder (ODD) can be best described as a repetitive emotive pattern, and this pattern should have lasted for at least six months to indicate that it is not an acute emotional outburst or an emotional issue that the child or teen had to deal with that is not typically related with a chronic condition. It is also directed specifically at authority figures in the child or teen's lives, who can be their parents, a coach, or an educator. Normally, there is no aggression involved as this behavior would point to another issue named conduct disorder. ODD is typically verbal and not normally physical at all. There is a list of symptoms, apart from the fact that their exhibition should be continued for a period of six months or longer that a child needs to be associated with for a possible diagnosis. Another detail that sets an ODD child or teen apart from a child exhibiting normal behavior is that one cannot seem to satisfy the child or teen's dissatisfaction or disdain with authority, authority figures, and nothing seems to make them happy.

Children younger than five are known to exhibit these types of defiant and argumentative behavior fairly often or even most days; in an older child, it may manifest at the very least twice a week. The main objective is to try and identify a pattern of behavior that is more intense and indicates a frequency that seems abnormal and has a high-intensity level compared to the behavior of a typical child. A functional way to measure the level of intensity of the child or teen's behavior is by looking for areas in their lives where this behavior is causing damage or impairment. For example, this ongoing tendency from your child or teen to cause conflict and object to authority may possibly make things very difficult at home. It can also cause a lot of trouble at school, which includes poor academic performance and ultimately social alienation and the loss of friends. It is not uncommon for children or teenagers with ODD to become socially marginalized in environments like at school. Although there is an estimate that about 3% of children suffer from ODD, medical professionals add that there is a strong possibility that the number is actually higher due to the fact that there may be many children and teenagers who have not been diagnosed with the condition.

The Physiological Development

Research has been conducted on the neurological aspects of children and teenagers who are diagnosed with ODD, and although no hard evidence was found, an open question remains among specialists about some neurobiological differences between children diagnosed with ODD and those who are not. An interesting research-based observation postulates that ODD is more prevalent in boys than in girls, only prior to the onset of puberty. However, after the onset of puberty, the number of cases start to even out between the sexes, with ODD affecting 9% of girls and 11% of boys. It is also said that the way symptoms are displayed is different between the sexes, which may be relevant to the general ways young girls and boys approach and handle different situations. There are studies indicating that some factors can make specific children more susceptible or likely to develop ODD than others. One of these factors that play a role in how likely a child or teen is to develop ODD or other conduct disorders is a genetic component. An interesting link is made between individuals diagnosed with mood disorders, ADHD, antisocial personality, and substance abuse disorders, and the likelihood of a first-degree relative (children) developing ODD. These are the physiological and neurological components of ODD that have thus far been discovered, but also in existence is a strong nature versus nurture argument which postulates that the manifestation of ODD occurs due to an interplay between genes and the environment the child or teenager is in. There is some encouraging news in statistical data, though, as an estimated two-thirds of children diagnosed with ODD will be able to deal with and overcome their destructive symptoms and behavior, and that when a child who is diagnosed with Oppositional Defiant Disorder reaches the age of 17, there is a 70% chance that this disorder will no longer be playing a dominating role in their life and that they will not be experiencing any symptoms of ODD.

Symptoms and Behavior

There are specific symptoms a parent should be on the lookout for if they suspect that their child or teenager may suffer from ODD. This list is quite extensive, but the child does not have to indicate signs of all the listed symptoms; as we previously mentioned, only four symptoms are required for a probable diagnosis. The symptoms on the list include situations where a child or teenager often loses their temper, or just as often annoyed and touchy for no apparent reason. These children also exhibit resentful attitudes and behavior and are often angry at authority figures or in situations where they have to follow rules. ODD symptoms also include a hostile and argumentative attitude towards any figure they may deem to be an authority figure, and if an authority figure makes a request, the child or teen will not comply with such a request, especially if it's related to rules or adhering to rules. If your child or teen often goes out of their way to deliberately annoy others and don't want to take ownership of their mistakes, these are also possible symptoms. ODD children and teens are known for blaming others when they get into trouble or when they are the focus of a disciplinary process. Finally, behavior that a concerned parent can look out for is spiteful and vindictive behavior. These types of behaviors do not necessarily happen so often; however, if you have observed them within the past six months, you can include it as a valid behavioral symptom. This diagnostic guide is based on the American Psychiatric Association's Diagnostic and Statistical Manual of Mental Disorders (DSM-5). Parents need to keep in mind that ODD symptoms may vary from person to person, so if you know someone whose kid has ODD and they behave in a specific way, try not to use the child as your parameter; use the provided set of symptoms instead. We are all different and when it comes to mental disorders, we may have the same issue but display the symptoms very differently. Especially in a case like this where a child or teen only requires four from the eight main symptoms for an initial consultation; this can cause different children with ODD's behavior to be very much the same but also different. When looking for these symptoms in your child, keep your child's personality and temperament in mind as well to ensure that you identify the symptoms authentically and contextually. Some cognitive symptoms that are very common with ODD include a child or teen's inability to speak before thinking, having a difficult time concentrating, and frequent bouts of frustration (Valley Behavioral Health System, 2017; Mayo Clinic, 2018).

Causes, Risk Factors, and C0-occurring Disorders

It is imperative to also discuss co-occurring disorders as these may be a precursor or an indication that a child may be more likely to develop ODD. The child themselves does not have to have one of these conditions but may have a closely-related family member that does. On the other hand, conditions or disorders that typically manifest later in life like Bipolar Disorder are more likely to happen to children or teens who show symptoms of ODD. It is important when evaluating a child or teen with ODD to also look for signs of other co-occurring disorders. These conditions include attention deficit hyperactivity disorder or ADHD, learning disabilities, depression, bipolar disorder as earlier mentioned, and anxiety disorders. If a coexisting condition can be identified and treated in tandem with the ODD symptoms, chances are that the treatment may be significantly more successful as these co-existing conditions often aggravate ODD in a child or teen as it causes even more difficulty, confusion, and frustration. There have also been cases with children and teens diagnosed with ODD progressing to developing conduct disorder, where the child would develop a pattern of violent and disruptive rebellious behavior. To understand ODD as a whole, one also needs to understand which other conditions a child or teen may have that can aggravate the symptoms.

Anxiety Disorder

Although experiencing anxiety is normal in a stressful situation, having anxiety disorder points to a situation where someone experiences this state of angst or fear to such a point that it becomes all-consuming and affects their well-being and their ability to live a normal life. A physiological anxiety response happens when your brain senses a threat and responds by releasing hormones that put your body in defense mode. Children and teens can experience anxiety at school if they have to prepare for a big test when they didn't do their homework and the teacher is busy checking everyone's work, if they are waiting for test results, or if they experience relationship insecurity with their friends. They can also experience anxiety at home if there are conflict situations between parents or siblings, the living situation is not stable, or if there are significant financial problems. However, these are all, although serious, normal reasons for a child to be anxious. When someone has an anxiety disorder, they may go through the same situations, but their level of anxiety is so high that it becomes overwhelming to them. A child or teenager with an anxiety disorder lives in a perpetual state of fear and anxiety, which causes them to avoid engaging in normal activities like going to school, socializing with friends, avoid situations where you need to go out in public because you don't want to face other people, and limit your communication with others, even your family.

Due to extensive research on the topic of anxiety disorders, several different types have been identified that may apply to younger individuals who may also have ODD. Firstly, there is what is called Generalized Anxiety Disorder, which is basically described as an excessive and unrealistic feeling of worry for what would normally be perceived as a situation that would not require that level of worry. Next, there is panic disorder, which includes feelings of anxiety and excessive worry, but is also specifically characterized by sudden feelings of overwhelming fear and panic which induces a panic attack. During a panic attack, an individual may experience palpitations, chest pain, have more difficulty breathing due to their experiencing chest pain, and they can also break out in a sweat. They experience a very high level of fear that dislocates them from their immediate surroundings and reality. The severity of this experience may sometimes lead to the individual feeling like they are having a heart attack or that they cannot inhale enough oxygen, which causes a choking experience.

Social anxiety disorder, also known as social phobia, is when you spend a lot of time premeditating and then excessively worry about everyday social situations. For example, from a child or teen's perspective, they will likely create a social scenario that may happen at school, picture the worst social outcome for them that would probably lead to embarrassment or shame, and then obsessively worry about this. Separation anxiety is another type of anxiety that specifically manifests in children, but the condition can actually be developed by anyone. After one of a child's parents passes, especially when they are still young, they may develop separation anxiety due to the fear of losing their other parent or any other family member. Although there is some legitimacy in such fear, especially after losing someone close to you, there are also individuals who experience an irrational fear when someone they love leaves or is not in their direct sight or contact. Additionally, anxiety can also be caused by certain prescription medications, so if your child is on meds, consult your doctor to find out about the side-effects of the drugs and whether it may be causing unnecessary anxiety that could be exacerbating a condition like ODD. Anxiety is not a monolithic concept or condition, so when you are looking for signs of heightened anxiety in your child's behavior, be sure to consider these different types, which may give you more insight (Lerche Davis, 2003).

Depressive Disorders

There are three major types of depressive disorders commonly diagnosed among children and teens, which include disruptive mood dysregulation disorder, major depressive disorder, and persistent depressive disorder or *dysthymia*. In general, the term depression is thrown around a lot and can be used to describe feelings or experiences that are not related to actual depressive disorders. Everyone, adults and youngsters alike, experience times when they feel down, which are most likely caused by events during their everyday life. However, in cases where a person does not have a depressive disorder, this experience of feeling 'down' will restore itself again and it is not seen as the person's normal way of feeling. For example, the word depression or "feeling depressed" is often used to describe a person's discouragement that results from an acute event that caused disappointment or loss. Depressive disorders involve a pattern of low mood levels that are interlinked with feelings of worthlessness and self-loathing. Depression in children is believed to have the same cause as depression in adults, which is a significant loss or deprivation early on in life.

Children who suffer from depressive disorders may not be as able as adults to articulate their emotional experiences, but when observing their behavior, these children or teens will most likely show poor academic performance, attempts to withdraw from society, and can even act out in a delinquent manner. Children and teenagers who suffer from a depressive disorder will appear more irritable or aggressive than sad, which is an important difference between adult and childhood depression. The behavior of children and teenagers who suffer from depressive disorders can manifest as overactive, aggressive, and antisocial behavior.

Firstly, disruptive mood dysregulation disorder usually starts manifesting between the ages of 6 and 10 years in children and is categorized by disruptive behavior and persistent irritability. This specific type of depressive disorder is closely related to ODD as their behavioral symptoms are so similar. Disruptive mood dysregulation disorder is also linked with ADHD and anxiety. The diagnosis for this type of depressive disorder can be made after the age of 6 or before the age of 18. When a patient moves into adulthood, this condition may evolve into unipolar disorder, which involves depression without any manifestations of mania, or anxiety disorder. Be advised never to attempt diagnosing your child with any condition without the support of a medical professional, but disruptive mood dysregulation disorder usually requires a combination of behaviors occurring simultaneously for 12 months without there being three months gone by where one behavior is missing. This is something you can observe in a doctor's absence. These behaviors are, firstly, aggressive outbursts disproportionate to the relevant situation and that can manifest in verbal and physical expressions of rage (these will most likely occur, on average, 3 times a week), then the child will also exhibit temper-based outbursts that appear to be inconsistent with the level of cognitive and emotional development for their age, and appearing angry and irritable most of the time. It is also important that the child's outbursts should be observed in 2 of the 3 settings they find themselves in daily, which are at school, at home, or in the presence of their peers.

A major depressive disorder is more common after puberty, but it can occur at any age. This type of depressive disorder is different from disruptive mood dysregulation disorder as it is characterized by a discrete depressive episode lasting about two weeks. If the disorder is not treated, remission may occur within 6-12 months. Recurrence risks are higher in children and teens who have had severe episodes, who have experienced an episode at a younger age, and for children who have had multiple depressive episodes. Signs of major depressive disorder can be identified if a child, firstly, feels sad or even tearful mostly every day for a period of two weeks, and secondly, if the child experiences a loss of interest in things they would normally enjoy doing, which can appear as an expression of high-level boredom. Along with these two main indicators, you may also come across symptoms like insomnia or hypersomnia, weight changes, which are mostly recorded as decreased weight in children, fatigue, difficulty concentrating, possible recurrent thoughts about death or suicide, and feelings of worthlessness or feeling rejected or disapproved of. Even a child experiencing guilt that is contextually inappropriate can be an indicator. Major depressive disorder in older children of an adolescent age can have harrowing effects like academic decline, substance abuse, and suicidal tendencies. Major depression in younger children and teens can cause them to fall behind academically and lose out on developing crucial relationships with their peers.

Persistent depressive disorder or dysthymia can be identified as a persistently irritable or depressed mood that usually lasts most of the day, on most days for more than a 1 year period. The condition also includes at least two of the following behavioral symptoms: feelings of hopelessness, insomnia or hypersomnia, fatigue, difficulty concentrating, low self-esteem, and either a decreased appetite or overeating.

For all of these types of depressive disorders that may manifest in childhood and adolescence, a clinical diagnosis is necessary for confirmation purposes. However, it is unavoidable to notice how much the symptoms from some of these types of depressive disorders, which are also regarded as possible co-occurring disorders, resemble symptoms of ODD. For example, most types indicate irritable behavior, and the first type we discussed, which is disruptive mood dysregulation disorder, lists symptoms such as aggression and behavior that can affect their social development. This may very well be why these disorders co-occur, and the potential influence and aggravating factors they may have on ODD needs to be explored so parents can have clarity on this topic. Let's first move on to another disorder that is mainly characterized to start showing symptoms in young adulthood, but has also been diagnosed and studied in children and teenagers (Coryell, 2020).

Bipolar Disorder

Bipolar disorder often starts as a major depressive disorder in children, and symptoms of bipolar disorder can start showing during mid-puberty through to the mid-twenties. It is important to know, though, that not all children who are diagnosed with a form of the depressive disorder will come to develop bipolar disorder even though this is a precursor. Bipolar disorder, although an important component as it is seen as a legitimate co-occurring disorder to ODD, is not at all common among children. Previous diagnoses of prepubescent children who showed unstable moods at an intense level were diagnosed with bipolar disorder, but this diagnosis has changed to disruptive mood dysregulation disorder due to the progression of the condition typically moving in the direction of a depressive disorder and not a subsequent, fully-blown bipolar disorder as the child gets older. The development of Bipolar Disorder may occur after puberty in the young adulthood of an individual who had ODD as a child and can be linked to ODD in this way.

Bipolar Disorder, from a behavioral or symptomatic perspective, is characterized by periods of mania, depression, and what can be perceived as a "normal mood." The requirement for diagnosis is that these states are constantly alternating and recurring and that they can last for weeks or months before transitioning to another state or mood. Treatment for Bipolar Disorder typically requires psychiatric drugs, but therapy is also recommended.

There is no concrete evidence about what causes Bipolar Disorder, but medical experts and researchers believe that there is definitely a genetic or hereditary component combined with the dysregulation of the neurotransmitters norepinephrine and serotonin, and also a likely contributing factor of a stressful life event.

When an adolescent goes through a manic period or episode, they may appear very positive, or even hyperirritable, and these moods can also alternate during a manic phase. They tend to go into a productivity overdrive, and their speech is noticeably rapid and driven. Their sleep patterns will change as they will start sleeping less and an inflated self-esteem or a grandiose self-perception will be noticeable. Mania can reach the point of psychosis, where the adolescent may lose touch with reality and may say things like they are God, they have supreme knowledge that no-one else has, and they will have a severely impaired sense of judgment that will lead to reckless and self-destructive behavior like casual sex, binge drinking, and even drug abuse. Because of the serious repercussions, a manic episode may have on an adolescent's life, monitoring the situation and seeking professional help is crucial. If your young child has ODD, you don't have to expect or fear a transition into Bipolar Disorder as they grow older; however, if you are aware of the prevalence of this disorder in relatives, you can help your child by conducting some preventive behavioral observation.

Intermittent Explosive Disorder

Intermittent explosive disorder is characterized by extreme and aggressive outbursts that can include impulsive, violent behavior, verbal outbursts, where the reaction does not fit the context of the situation at all. It is usually observed as a gross overreaction that is blown completely out of proportion to the situation it is linked with. In adults, examples of intermittent explosive disorder include road rage, domestic abuse, attempting to throw or break objects in your proximity, or extreme temper tantrums. The condition is classified as chronic, and a child can show symptoms of this disorder for years, although the severity of the episodes or outbursts will decrease as the individual gets older.

The symptoms of the intermittent explosive disorder can be quite unsettling to someone who has never experienced an outburst like this before. A completely authentic episode can develop and erupt within the timespan of 30 minutes, completely without warning. What makes this disorder more tricky to diagnose is that these outbursts can be separated by weeks or even by months of non-violent and non-aggressive behavior, which can make it look like an isolated incident. It can also be the case that the main outbursts tend to be physically aggressive and that they are interval led with verbal outbursts, which appear less serious. A person with intermittent explosive disorder can be chronically angry, irritated, and generally impulsive. An outburst or episode can be either accompanied or preceded (or both) by a tight feeling in one's chest, tremors and palpitations, a tingling feeling under the skin, a sudden surge of energy, racing thoughts, and rage or irritability. Has your child ever experienced any of these symptoms? Verbal and physical outbursts are usually accompanied by shouting, temper tantrums, heated arguments, the shoving or slapping of others, vandalism or causing property damage, and threats to harm people or animals. After the episode or outburst is over, the child or individual may experience a sense of relief, and they will feel physically tired. At a later stage, they will experience shame, remorse, guilt, regret, or embarrassment.

There are multiple causes for intermittent explosive disorder, and they can act in on each other. This means that the disorder seldomly has a singular cause. The first component that can cause intermittent explosive disorder is, as with most disorders, genetics. Genetics are not often ruled out as a causal factor when it comes to mental disorders, and if there is a family member, specifically a direct family member who has also shown symptoms or received a diagnosis for this specific disorder, this is a valid reason to keep your eyes peeled. The other frequently present contributing factor is the environment. As environmental factors cannot ever be ruled out entirely when looking at the cause of mental illness, it will also remain a potential causal component. However, there are specific environmental circumstances that are isolated and emphasized in this case, which includes physical and verbal abuse. Exposure to this type of harmful behavior at a young age can trigger the intermittent explosive disorder. Finally, a child can develop intermittent explosive disorder due to differences in brain function, brain chemistry, and brain structure. This statement is only based on observations and, although the idea is completely conceivable, concrete evidence has yet to be produced. Finally, two risk factors that link with these causes provide a reason to keep you alert as a parent for this disorder. They are, firstly, if the child has suffered physical abuse, and secondly if the child has been diagnosed or shows signs of other mental disorders.

Children with intermittent explosive disorder will ultimately struggle to form meaningful relationships, they will experience inconsistencies and trouble with their mood and, as a consequence, they will experience difficulties at school and at home. If the condition is untreated, they may resort to self-harm, and they can develop other health issues such as diabetes, heart problems, high blood pressure, and experience physical pain (Mayo Clinic, 2020).

Intellectual Developmental Disorder

Intellectual developmental disorder, also known as IDD, is more of a newly discovered and labeled as a neuro-developmental disorder where the symptoms and characteristics were previously placed under the same umbrella as what was then called "mental retardation." However, IDD is not a full manifestation of mental disability, so the disorder was given its own identity and is now identified as a mental disorder.

The key components of the intellectual developmental disorder are linked to a child having certain developmental deficits or shortcomings when it comes to specific intellectual processes and intellectual functioning. These functions include proper reasoning, effective judgment, planning, abstract thinking, and they can have difficulty with learning in general.

A child with IDD's learning processes is remarkably slower than a child who is considered to have no impairments in this regard. The signs or symptoms of this disorder can be observed in multiple stages of a child's development. For example, children with IDD may have trouble starting crawling and standing up and they may only do this successfully much later than other children. Their vocal abilities are also likely to develop later, and as they become old enough to go to school, problems may occur in the classroom as they tend to struggle with clear communication and will find it difficult to interpret and apply new information that is presented to them. A child with IDD will struggle to keep up with their peers in school due to the slower processing of information and their inability to understand some concepts. They will, for example, not have the ability to develop problem-solving skills, they can indicate a lack of social inhibitions or an understanding of how social norms work. In this case, though, they do so because they do not understand social boundaries as opposed to a rebellious child purposefully crossing social boundaries. A child that has IDD can struggle with everyday tasks that other children will see as completely normal, like giving someone the correct change, following cooking instructions, or organizing the items in the pantry.

The risk factors for IDD include genes or genetic syndromes, malformations occurring in the brain of the child, the influence of drugs or alcohol during pregnancy, traumatic brain injury, complications during labor, types of seizure disorders, and even severe social deprivation. The diagnosis for IDD includes an IQ test, where a score below 70 can be an indication that the child may have IDD. However, this IQ score is not enough for a comprehensive diagnosis; the child needs to be observed to see if there are other adaptive or communication issues present. It is assumed that this disorder is already present before birth, except if the child suffers physical trauma or a toxic exposure before they reach the age of 18 (Child Mind Institute, 2020a).

Language Disorder

Children who have language disorder generally struggle with both understanding and speaking a language, usually their native language. Language disorder is not the same as speech sound disorder; however, the two can be confused. Speech sound disorder concerns problematic sound production.

Language disorder can be described as a communication disorder where a child experiences constant issues with language use as well as language acquisition. For example, a child can struggle to process specific linguistic information like sentence structure, vocabulary, and discourse. The disorder affects a child's ability to process and produce language and also forms of communication, may they be spoken, written, or even gestural. Children with language disorders do not, however, have any trouble producing speech sounds.

If your child has language disorder, symptoms have most likely manifested from a very early stage in their childhood; however, you will only realize this later when their functioning requires more complex linguistic processing. A child that has language disorder will usually have issues with comprehending and processing what other people say, especially compared to the speed of comprehension of a child that does not have language disorder. This disorder can cause the child to leave out words from a sentence when speaking, use placeholders like 'um' a lot while they search for words when speaking, and they tend to repeat or echo parts of questions, whole questions, and use incorrect tenses often. These children appear shy as they are reluctant to talk because it is a difficult process for them.

If you are aware of family members or ancestors that had language disorder, this can be a reason to keep your eyes peeled and be more vigilant for symptoms. A diagnosis requires a child to have problems or deficits in communication that is deemed appropriate for their age, affecting their vocabulary, sentence structure, and if they have trouble using the correct language to transfer information in a conversation. The most effective treatment for language disorder is speech therapy and can be accompanied by cognitive behavior therapy and psychotherapy (Child Mind Institute, 2020b).

Conduct Disorder

Conduct disorder is often mistaken for oppositional defiant disorder. However, if one looks at the symptoms, there are some surprising differences that will have you wondering why you compared them in the first place. Nonetheless, it's best to know what conduct disorder is as this will help you understand the symptoms of your child's ODD. Here is a lowdown of the most important characteristics, tendencies, and behaviors associated with children who have conduct disorder.

Conduct disorder or the prevalence thereof affects about 10% of children, and the symptoms most commonly start to show in late childhood to early adolescence. This disorder is also more common in boys than in girls, and it is different from oppositional defiant disorder due to its significantly higher level of violent behavior. The definition of conduct disorder is a pattern, described as persistent or recurrent, of behavior that violates the rights of other individuals and also violates age-appropriate societal norms or rules.

Although genetics is not ruled out as a causal factor for this disorder, a heavy emphasis is placed on the child's home environment, and that if a child's parents regularly participate in substance abuse or have been diagnosed with disorders like schizophrenia, ADHD, mood disorders, or an antisocial personality disorder, this can be a strong indicator to the cause of conduct disorder development. This being said, it is not completely uncommon for a child growing up in what would be perceived as a healthy and high-functioning household to develop conduct disorder. So, what makes conduct disorder different from oppositional defiant disorder or ODD? Here are some signs to look for, though I don't think you'd have to look very hard.

A child with conduct disorder doesn't have the ability to empathize with others in terms of their well-being and emotions and they can easily interpret another child or adult's behavior as intentionally threatening even if there are no indications of a threat whatsoever. Children with conduct disorder want to cause damage and do so by acting aggressively, bullying others, conducting acts of physical cruelty on others, displaying and using weapons, forcing another into taking part in a sexual act, and they have no feelings of regret or remorse for their actions. They will likely divert their aggression and cruelty toward animals, and they have no issue lying, stealing, or vandalizing property. They do not tolerate rules and are likely to run away from home or stay away from school.

Although boys are more likely to have conduct disorder than girls, there is still a notable difference in their symptoms which can be valuable knowledge to have. On the one hand, boys are more likely to vandalize, steal, and fight, which points to more physical conduct issues. On the other hand, girls are prone to run away from home, tell lies, and get involved in prostitution. Both sexes are likely to use illicit drugs and can have suicidal tendencies. It is crucial for any suicidal tendencies or suicide attempts to be taken very seriously in these cases (Elia, 2019).

Complications

There are serious effects from undiagnosed and untreated ODD that can cause permanent damage to your child's life. Early detection, although not always possible because of the six-month time span required for the detection of any legitimate initial signs, is crucial for the well-being of the child or teen because, as the condition becomes more severe, it will lead to serious complications in their lives that can last until adulthood. These complications include social issues like a loss or a complete lack of friendships and close relationships, the subsequent inability to develop any sort of meaningful relationships, they can go through life experiencing social isolation, and while they attend an educational institution, this setting will most likely be difficult for them to adjust to and to function in. If ODD goes on untreated and the child or teen transitions into adulthood, issues may persist and even show further development. For example, such an individual would indicate an ongoing pattern of broken relationships and relationship conflicts, they would typically try to control those around them, which is one of the causes of their social alienation and isolation. Another is undeniably such an individual's inability to let go of a grudge or being unable to forgive someone, which can also completely destroy a relationship. And then, when these defiant little ones grow up, they still don't deal well with authority figures, and this time it may cost them their jobs or they may end up in a jail cell (Valley Behavioral Health System, 2017; Mayo Clinic, 2018).

How to Process this Information Overload

This chapter has provided a myriad of information about mental disorders, starting with the main topic of discussion, which is oppositional defiant disorder, and then moving on to a lengthy discussion of potential co-occurring conditions or disorders that are or have been associated with ODD. So, what do we as concerned parents need to make of all this information? Some of the symptoms discussed in a few of the co-occurring conditions like mood disorders and intermittent explosive disorder can seem downright frightening, and they can make you fear for your child's health and sanity. However, the purpose of the first chapter is to lay all the facts about ODD bare, so the rest of the guide can continue based on information. This chapter is synonymous with the mantra "knowledge is power" and aims to arm you with the most up-to-date information out there that may help you and your child. There is one golden rule when going through these details, especially from a parent's perspective. We know how protective we are of our children. Don't mix knowledge or information with emotion, or worse, paranoia or neuroticism. Chapter 1 is your toolbox where you can read up on and find information about different components that may contribute to your child's condition. Yet, it is extremely important that you don't diagnose your child yourself based on this information; if you know that your child has ODD but you suspect that there may be another disorder lurking in the background, the best thing you can do for your child is taking them to a therapist or psychiatrist and tell the medical professional about your observations. Feel empowered by everything you've read so far. In the next chapter, we're focusing on you, your power as a human being, and how you can manifest your strength in a way that will benefit your whole family.

Chapter 2: Did I do This?

The most prevalent observation that parents who have children with ODD have shared with me is that, when their little ones were still babies and toddlers, they thought that the behavior must be a phase and that it shall pass. When their children got older and started socializing with other children, they realized that their children's behavior were starkly different from other children's, and there's even an account from one mother who used to think her son's behavior was just a type of gender-related behavioral difference in comparison to how her daughter behaved said that, when she observed her son playing with other boys for the first time, she realized that his behavior is not typical of a little boy or any normal child his age. She said that she could immediately see that there is something wrong with her son's behavior and that his 'intentions' in the way he plays were different than with the other boys. Parents fear not only for their children's future, but in some cases for their lives, and one cannot blame a parent for wanting to do introspection in an attempt to find out if they could have been the cause of their child's debilitating issues. If you are in the process of doing this or often dwell on these thoughts, it is a clear indication that you deeply care for your child and that the only issue may be that you don't have the necessary resources or information to know which steps to take. The first step you can take toward helping your child is to get rid of any feelings of guilt or self-loathing you are currently harboring due to witnessing your child or teen's suffering. You may even feel a sense of resentment toward your child because of their perpetual rejection and disdain for your efforts, which is not only a crucial emotion that needs to be dealt with but also a contextual situation within a parent-child relationship that involves ODD that requires acceptance and understanding. Let's take the first steps toward healing. Self-healing and self-acceptance will have an amazing effect on your child or teen.

Why You Shouldn't Blame Yourself

One of the things a parent with a child who has ODD needs to realize is that, because their child's behavior is irrational and non-accomodating, they may not have as much control over what they say or do as you may want to believe. Their behavior may even be impulsive, which means that they've given it no thought before acting out. This doesn't mean that their behavior doesn't wreak havoc in the household, can cause psychological issues for siblings, instigate marital issues, or leave you with an eventual sense of complete defeat and even developing depression. A caring parent always feels responsible for the way their child behaves and conducts themselves because you taught them to behave that way, right? So, what did you do wrong this time? What did you do to hurt your child on such a level that they display such hatred and scorn? Raising a child with a mental disorder must be one of life's most painful and difficult journeys.

Taking a step back and realizing that focusing on your health is even more crucial now that you have a child that is mentally struggling is hard to understand when you are stuck in a pattern of anxiety, guilt, and that overwhelming feeling of hopelessness. It can feel like a bottomless pit, and you can't recall when you fell into it, nor do you know how to get out. If there is one source of inspiration for you to get your mental health back on track, let it be the health of your child or teen who is struggling with their own, as two sick individuals are not going to solve the issue, especially if one is the caregiver. Let's look at a typical day of a parent who raises a child with ODD:

The first potential conflict situation you as the parent most likely expect is getting your child or teen ready for school. Getting them out of bed if they still want to sleep, making sure they have dressed appropriately (especially the teens), and trying to encourage them to eat a semi-nutritious breakfast if they feel like eating at all is enough to make you want to go back to bed and bury your head under the covers. However, instead of internalizing their negative behavior, focus on keeping your demeanor positive and firm but friendly. Separate yourself from your child's destructive attempts even though you know that they need validation and attention. You can give it to them without allowing yourself to go through an emotional ordeal every time they have a violent outburst. But let's face it, it's all easy on black and white, but if you're in that situation, it's like standing in the ocean, overcome by multiple currents of emotions trying to carry you in all different directions. While it is overwhelming, dizzying, I know you have what it takes to keep your head above water. It will take time, effort, and most of all, patience. You are more than capable of doing it. So, to start somewhere, you need tools and knowledge. Every chapter is going to provide you with knowledge. Let's look at how you can preserve your sanity, understand your thought processes, and manage them effectively without experiencing any further guilt by, firstly, thinking proactive thoughts.

The Importance of the 3 P's

Parenting is not the only crucial and relevant word that starts with a capital 'P' when you are raising a child or teen with ODD. There are other P's that work well with parenting, especially if you need strength, mental endurance, and the ability to understand that you can get through this. In fact, there are three main P's that every parent who lives with an ODD child or teen needs to know about, understand, and internalize; Positivity, Proactivity, and Patience. Now, whether you are at your wits' end at this point or just starting your journey with your ODD cub, we're going to take the three P's slow and steady so they can sink in and your body absorbs their energy like a thirsty sponge.

Positivity

If you want to look after your child and help your child cope and manage their disorder, you need to look after yourself. The word positivity is thrown around a lot, and sometimes in a fashion and in situations where it can be very inappropriate. For example, after a family member has passed, you don't want some chump punching you in the shoulder and saying, "Look on the bright side, granny's in heaven now." Sure, that may be true, but the nature of the communication was far removed from genuine positivity. This patronizing approach is not the main idea for this discussion. True positivity doesn't mean you always have to crack a smile and answer yes to everything or that worrying about something in your life makes you negative. True positivity makes you stronger so you can ultimately make the best decisions with an open and unclouded mind when you are in difficult situations. True positivity has a lot to do with your relationship with yourself and how you keep this relationship healthy. To help your child develop a healthy mind, you need to nurture and maintain one yourself. So, before we look at the main ways to make that positivity shift, let's look at what a positive mind can offer you according to research:

One of the most important benefits of a positive mind is a healthy body. If you are positively inclined, you tend to avoid stressing about unnecessary things and you will most likely have a high level of overall well-being. A benefit that goes with having a healthy body due to a positive outlook is that your immune system also gets a boost and is stronger in general. A study was conducted to test the power of the mind on the effects of the flu vaccine. What researchers found was quite astonishing–activation in areas of the brain that are associated with negativity lead to the individual having a weaker immune response to a flu vaccine. A similar outcome was recorded in related research as researchers noted that individuals who slid more towards the optimistic side of the scale when it came to important events in their lives tended to naturally have healthy immune responses, or healthier than their pessimistic counterparts. Other health benefits that have reportedly been linked with a positive or optimistic outlook include improved cardiovascular health, a longer lifespan, and a decreased risk of being depressed or being diagnosed with depression. Researchers cannot provide a direct or detailed physiological explanation for why a certain type of thinking would lead to better health, but there is an abundance of research-based proof. It has been proposed that positive individuals tend to naturally live healthier lifestyles than their pessimistic counterparts, which could be part of the explanation.

Another benefit you will get from positivity is building a protective wall of resilience around yourself. When you've come to that point where you are able to stay resilient against any attacks or events that can turn you back to pessimism, you come to see that positivity and resilience goes hand-in-hand. It's the positivity that makes us resilient, and that resilience, when applied, helps us to stay sane and positive through difficult times. Researchers have found that, in times where people have experienced extreme hardships like being the victims of terrorist attacks, some people respond by showing a natural resilience toward depression and defeat that keeps them thriving and helps people to move forward. However, this natural resilience can also be developed in individuals who do not have the ability to produce this superpower when they need it. A great discovery made by researchers is that resilience and positivity can be cultivated within a human being, whether they have a natural affinity or potential for it or not. And, if you feel like you don't have this potential, that doesn't mean that you are not a strong individual. You can arm yourself with the knowledge that, by nurturing positive emotions and by making them a priority during troubling times, you will be able to reap short-term and long-term benefits from your state of mind, even if you are not able to see this right from the beginning. Some of the benefits that can also contribute to changing your life for the better are an improved ability to manage your stress levels, decreasing levels of depressed feelings or depression itself, and learning and building a new custom set of coping skills that can help you deal with troubling situations and crises even better in the future.

After taking all of this in, researchers also find it imperative for people to know that positivity and optimism needs to be applied realistically. Now, after what you've just read, it probably sounds like they want to suddenly tell you to forget everything they've said. However, what they are referring to is a type of "blind optimism," where you are so focused on being positive and excessively optimistic that you lose the ability to identify problems you have to deal with, which may be crucial issues in your household. Being excessively optimistic can lead you to overestimate your ability to handle crisis and difficult situations, which will make you take on more than you can handle and ultimately bring you back to step one, which is where you are struggling under a mountain of anxiety and stress. Excessive positivity or optimism can be described as ignoring reality in favor of the "silver lining," where true positivity is more about identifying and trying to make the best of bad situations by believing in your abilities and taking a positive approach when you encounter a challenge.

Now that we've looked at the benefits of positive thinking, it may also be beneficial to define it and discuss its methods and characteristics. Firstly, as we can tell from the previous discussion, positive thinking is not about avoiding the bad and the ugly in the world. It focuses on how you approach these negative aspects. Positive thinking is an admirable quality because it is a strength; it is the ability to make the most out of a situation that others would regard as fruitless or redundant. Have you ever felt that way in your life? Most of us have been in situations where we felt like that countless times. The same applies when you look at other people. Do you only see their flaws or do you try to see the potential in them? If you think about your child and their struggles with ODD, this is a situation that not only affects you directly but mostly in a negative way. Is it hard for you to look past your child's behavior and identify their potential? Or, does it sometimes feel that there is a complete void of potential? Focusing on your own positive behavior can affect the behavior of others because the final part of positivity is being positive about yourself. This is a very powerful emotional tool, especially if you have children as they will grow up with a parent or parents who value themselves instead of constantly nitpicking on their own faults and shortcomings. Projecting positivity is invaluable therapy that you, as a parent, can provide for a child that struggles with a frustrating disorder (Cherry, 2012).

Proactivity

Proactivity or proactive behavior is normally associated with business and employee behavior and training, but this concept and what it entails is actually applicable to all aspects of life and how we approach them. A basic definition of proactive behavior is taking action and making a change instead of waiting to react to a situation after it has taken place. This means that, if you anticipate a situation, the proactive approach would be to take initiative and control the outcome instead of reacting to the outcome which was then controlled by someone or something else. When I said 'reacting' to the outcome, I was referring to the behavior opposite to proactive behavior, which is reactive behavior. Reactive behavior is associated with a pessimistic frame of mind, where an individual will wait for something to happen even though they had the power to influence or change it, and then blame it on an external source or individual. This is that kind of throwing your hands up in the air after something has happened and saying, "Well, what could I have done? They should've done something" attitude. That being said, there is no way you can possibly control or influence every situation in the world, so the idea of proactivity should be applied while keeping that in mind. However, if you do get that nagging feeling that you should have jumped in and changed the way things turned out, then there most probably was an opportunity for you to be proactive. The point of discussing proactivity is also for us to learn how to identify new situations that can benefit from our proactivity in ways we never thought possible. In this context, I'm referring to parenting, running a household, and dealing with a child or teen that has a disruptive disorder. Proactivity can become a powerful component of how we handle violent and emotional outbursts and balance family life for all family members even though there are difficult circumstances.

There are three keywords that describe proactive behavior to a tee. The first one is *anticipatory*. This is basically taking what we've discussed above and putting it into one word; when a person acts in advance of a certain situation instead of waiting to react at the end. From a household perspective, you can use a very simple example where most parents are proactive: you'd buy new groceries before every crumb in the house is finished instead of waiting until your family is going hungry and then going to the closest Walmart. The second keyword that describes proactivity describes a higher level of thinking that is involved with this concept, and that word is *change-oriented*. Being change-oriented has a lot to do with taking control of a situation, especially when it comes to the outcome. We are most likely to adapt to situations, and this is not a bad quality at all, especially if you are not on your own territory. However, being able to discern when you can act in a change-oriented way and when it is required is part of being a proactive individual, and you most certainly have the right to do so in your own household. That brings us to the third keyword that seals the deal for proactivity, and it is *self-initiated*. A proactive individual does not need to be instructed to act; they instinctively know when they can apply action to change the course of a situation for the better. This keyword also suggests that proactive behavior contains an element of leadership. If you have the courage and the will to initiate change, you are a leader and you have the ability to lead your family into a positive environment where they can feel safe and loved, even if the threat of destabilization comes from within. As a proactive parent, you will have the ability to initiate a different, more positive approach in your household if you see that the current one is not productive. Proactivity is ultimately empowering, especially if you make choices that initiate positive change, stick with them, and start to see results.

Being a proactive parent means that you know your child has to experience life's challenges and go through them to become a richer, wiser individual but also realizing when you need to step in if your troubled child needs help or causes disruption that affects other members of the household. Proactivity is tightly linked with positivity because the proactive choices you make should essentially be positive and have the intent to create a positive environment. In the next chapter, which is about the different types of treatment, you'll read about different ways your ODD child or teen can be treated through therapy, and that there is a specific no-nonsense approach where the parent or caregiver is taught to give no response whatsoever to an act of aggression by completely ignoring the child. This may seem like a negative approach, but the tricky part is to see the positivity in the big picture by knowing that, even though you need to ignore toxic behavior, you can provide positive reinforcement for productive behavior and envelope your child in an environment of support, love, and care.

Proactive parenting strategies also consist of three guidelines. First, you choose what you think will work for you and your child related to the unique situation you find yourselves in. Not only should you choose something that will work for you, but it should also feel right; it shouldn't go in against your values or beliefs. Finally, what you choose should fit in with your ODD child or teen's temperament, and your rules. When I say that it should fit in with your child's temperament, that doesn't necessarily mean it should support your child's aggressive and toxic behavior. However, choosing a method that will exacerbate their condition will not improve the situation either (A Conscious Rethink, 2019; PROactive Parenting, 2020)

Patience

Patience is not only related to parenting. Unfortunately, this aspect is related to all components of our lives, and some of us are just born with less patience. I know I am. However, sometimes, something or someone just crosses your path that gently forces you to develop this life-changing skill, and suddenly, everything becomes easier! Some people learn faster than others as I know some elderly individuals who have never learned how to master the art of patience. Patience really is a virtue, and it is something that you as a person control and can use to control how much of your energy you want to waste on situations that are out of your control. This is the last of the 3 P's, and with very good reason. By mastering the skill of patience, you can overcome obstacles in your life you never thought possible and have a most surprisingly positive effect on those around you.

Now, for parents specifically, patience is not only a virtue, it is a must-have. A definition of patience is a person's ability or capacity to bear pain or difficult situations without complaining and with a sense of calmness. Do you agree with this definition of patience? If you think about how you feel in situations where patience is so badly needed, this definition sounds so oversimplified—almost like it's very easy to act that way. To remain calm and to stand your ground in the face of a defiant child or teenager can really test this skill. However, if your reaction is to lose your temper or to complain, then these avenues will place even more stress on you and will not solve the problem. A lack of patience and its effects can have the opposite effect you are aiming for and can lead to feelings of anger and resentment in you and the other members of your family.

Patience, firstly, is a priceless aid that helps you to deal with those everyday issues and problems in a calm and rational way, which is the most effective way to deal with any annoying, irritating issues that unexpectedly tries to ruin your day. Patience can help you see small issues for what they are and help you to stay focused on the bigger picture, which, for a parent, may be the well-being and happiness of every member in the household. Finally, patience is vital for dealing with a crisis situation. Without the ability to be patient, it is unlikely that you'll be able to stay calm and maintain emotional stability during a stressful event, which can affect your children emotionally.

The good news is that it is possible to increase your levels of patience because patience is not only an attitude but also an ability. And, these are both things that we as humans can change. The problem is if your household is constantly in a crisis situation, which is often the case if you live with a child or teen that has ODD, when and where will you find the time to develop the level of patience required to manage a household that is constantly being disrupted by one of the members?

First, something we're not always aware of as parents but that plays a major role in family dynamics are our attitudes. This includes not only the attitude you hold about your family but also the attitude you hold about yourself. It's all about what you believe you can and cannot do. That's why it is commonly believed that one's attitude and self-belief can be a self-fulfilling prophecy. Interestingly enough, a prominent psychologist, Dr. Carol Dweck identified two types of mindsets, one being a growth mindset and one being a fixed mindset. A fixed mindset is the type of mindset where you tend to be reactive instead of proactive; where you sit and wait for things to happen instead of making them happen, while the growth mindset is wired to get their hands dirty and make the changes themselves. This has more to do with attitude than patience, but attitude is directly linked to patience. So, imagine that your attitude towards yourself and your family resembles a fixed mindset. Your mindset, just like your attitude, can make or break the way you do things and the effect it has on the people around you. It's almost like a self-fulfilling prophecy, and you are the prophet. For example, if you truly believe that you are failing as a parent and that you don't have the ability to be patient, your behavior will continue to follow patterns that will only frustrate you and cause you more stress. This type of attitude will dramatically decrease the effectiveness of any approach you follow to try and fix the situation, and your self-confidence as a parent will drop. Ultimately, if you feel that you have inadequate parenting skills, you will struggle more to find viable solutions to the problems that are testing your patience in the first place, and this is based solely on the fact that you believe you are unable to do so.

When it comes to attitudes, you can combine your approach to patience with a careful focus on your attitude toward your children and how you display these attitudes. For example, if your attitude towards your children is that they are purposefully trying to make your life miserable and that they are out to get you, this will have a direct impact on how long your patience will last with them. On the other hand, if you believe that they are making mistakes like all children do, and children need to do this in order to learn, this is an approach that will encourage more patience and, subsequently, help you to work constructively with misbehavior.

Some great advice for parents that want to work on being more patient is to, whenever you want to lose your temper, think long-term. For example, what will you gain in the long term from acting out now? Is there a better way to handle this situation? I think we as parents do understand long-term ideas and goals in parenting, but our ability to focus on and encourage long-term change and processes are interrupted by acute and disruptive occurrences or actions that appear to destroy any signs of long-term progress.

So, here we are at the important part of the discussion. How can you develop your patience as a parent? Especially if you have a child or teen that exhibits constant disruptive and possibly aggressive behavior in your household and in other parts of their lives? You, as a parent with a struggling child, can learn the art of patience the same way any other parent can, but you need to take smaller steps and focus on yourself and your sense of self-worth specifically through the process. While I was raising my child with ODD, I had serious issues with my self-esteem, and I also struggled to believe in myself as a parent. However, only later did I realize that these negative thoughts about myself were holding me back and keeping me and my child from developing a strong relationship and creating a safe home environment. And, they were directly influencing the amount of patience I had when my child acted out. I would immediately be engulfed in a fit of dismay, and instead of being the strong support system my child needed, I was the weak one that was unable to maintain sight of my child's long-term goal: to grow up as a healthy and happy adult.

So, the first and most important thing you need to do to develop patience and strength as a parent is to look after yourself and take care of your personal and emotional needs. Patient people are more relaxed and they are more prone to enjoying themselves–that's something that is very important in a household where there is constant tension and disagreement. Remember that self-care is important, and try to get your nightly rest.

A patient parent will choose a neutral approach when faced with a problem, which means that there is no impulsive response, and they avoid instinctive responses in situations of conflict as well. This is because, when being confronted with a conflict situation, a natural instinctive reaction will be self-defense, and your child may interpret this as an attack. It's best to take things as slow as possible. Allow yourself to calm down when you experience a conflict situation to enable a neutral approach. Patient parents will also develop their own effective problem-solving methods by inspecting a problem from different angles and considering all possible solutions before making a move. This often leads them to creative and individual solutions that are unique to the needs of their families and that works best with their family dynamics. Finally, here are four steps you can choose to follow or apply to your own parenting style that can help you develop a patient approach mindfully and gradually without losing your patience about not becoming more patient!

First, a very good nugget of advice is for you to do some introspection and figure out what triggers you as a parent. Isn't this the start of all conflicts? It's that trigger point, and you may surprise yourself when you start doing some deep thinking that there really are triggers your children know about but that you've never actively identified. A child or teen with ODD is also likely to use your trigger points as a tool for expressing their frustration and aggression. And, if it worked once, they'll do it again. So, think of a typical conflict situation between you and your child and try to pinpoint at which point exactly did you lose your temper. While doing this, don't focus on what your child did but on how you felt when you got triggered. That's the trigger point that's keeping you from developing a patient attitude. For example, was it a feeling of embarrassment that made you lose your temper? Alternatively, did you feel a pang of guilt about something that caused the anger and defense to flare up? Even sensations of hunger or being tired can be valid triggers. Knowing, acknowledging, and accepting your trigger points will keep you from reacting unnecessarily when your child tries to provoke you as you will know that your emotional response is engineered and planned so you can have the outburst, which your child sees as a valid response.

After you've done this little bit of introspection, you can shift your focus to observing your response to your child's behavior. Observe your physical response by focusing on your breathing, the thoughts that go through your mind, your anxiety levels, and your body temperature. What do you think when you get triggered? For example, "She KNOWS that I need to put Johnny to bet at 7 p.m., but she will STILL try and fight with me for not giving her any attention." When you start experiencing these thoughts of frustration, your mind takes on an "all or nothing" approach, which means that it is only thinking in extremes and there is not space for moderate considerations. For example, "Why is she ALWAYS late?" Is she always late, or are you just triggered? That's your brain going into extremes mode. If you can identify this when it happens, you can consciously slow down your thought process until you are in a more rational mode, which leads us to the third step in Operation Patience: devise a plan to manage your triggers.

Recognition and acknowledgment should be the hardest aspects of this exercise, except if you are a naturally introspective person who always reflects on their thoughts and actions. Devising a plan is our next step, and the outcome will be based on whatever you identified in step 1 and 2. A great format for such a plan is for it to have different components that address different parts of the triggering process. For example, let's create a plan with a preventive strategy, an "in the moment" strategy, and a review strategy.

Your preventive strategy can include aspects like when you can allow yourself time to relax, whether you want to count to ten before you respond when you encounter a difficult situation or any other proactive rules you want to set in place to improve the way you manage a difficult situation in the future.

Your "in the moment" strategy may be more focused on what you shouldn't do if you are suddenly confronted with a triggering situation. For example, you can make yourself a rule that, when triggered, to not immediately respond to whatever was being said or done. This will give you time to calm down and pull yourself together.

The review strategy can involve using every relevant event as a tool to improve your approach and response. Look back at how you handled a triggering event at home. Did you stay calm like you wanted to or did you lose your temper? By actively reviewing each component, you can make sure that you handle the next situation better and, in the process, develop the formidable skill of patience (Rowden, 2020; Steinkraus, 2015).

Work as a Team

When you have an ODD child or teen, they are likely to feel like they don't belong in the family because they are different from their siblings, their peers, their cousins, or whoever they compare themselves to. A great way to include them in family activities is to make sure the family uses teamwork as a common method to get things done. A family working together consists of individuals, each with their own strengths and weaknesses that come together as a unit, where those strengths and weaknesses can be balanced out and used effectively. This also applies to parents as a separate component in the family unit; parents that value teamwork and that work well as a team have a significantly positive impact on their children in terms of how they process emotions and how they approach relationships. Siblings who are encouraged to work as a team usually develop strong familial and friendship bonds as they feel a need to take care of each other and to look out for each other. The younger a family starts implementing and valuing teamwork, the better.

Considering these points, it's no surprise that the main definition for teamwork, whether it's in the context of a family or maybe from a work point of view, is more than one or multiple persons working together in order to achieve a common goal. If you look at the definition of teamwork this way, then you as parents need to set goals that the family can work towards as a team. What are the common goals that can help build a healthy family unit and healthy individuals within the family unit? They may include long-term goals like raising children to be successful adults, and in the shorter term, keeping all family members healthy and fit, relationship building, teaching the kids about financial management, and other skills they may need as grown-ups. Teamwork is a concept that is used a lot in business and has been studied and developed to improve the way employees cooperate to meet the main goals of a corporation. And, interestingly enough, many of these principles or concepts also apply to the way a family can approach successful and sustainable team building.

One of the most important aspects of team building that is also applicable in a family context is that all members of the family should share a common vision–the reason why they are working as a team. Not only should there be a shared goal, but trust should be highly regarded and cultivated at all times between family members. In this case, it is important to teach your children the importance of honesty and trust and to be approachable if they need to discuss anything with you that is bothering them. Encouraging openness and honesty will cultivate a culture of trust in your family.

Another crucial skill that you as a parent can develop with your partner and teach your children from a young age is to practice productive communication and conflict resolution. This is important in a household where one of the family members' behavior is disruptive and goes against these principles. Empower the siblings if there are any and help them to set an example for how to communicate effectively and without aggression towards each other and with you and your partner. An important part of effective communication that you can teach your children and discuss with your partner is to focus on developing listening skills. By actively listening to what someone is saying to you, you can identify deeper wants and needs. In Chapter 5, we'll be discussing communication with your ODD child and teen in-depth as effective communication and developed communication skills can make such a difference in a child's or adolescent's life.

As a parent or as parents, it is important to be aware that each member of the team has their own unique leadership abilities, even if they are struggling with a disorder. Your job is to identify these abilities in them and to empower them by showing each of your children that you notice these qualities and that there is a use for each of them in the family context. For example, let's say your youngster with ODD has great problem-solving abilities. You can empower your child by asking them for help when you encounter minor issues that require problem-solving skills on their level. This type of emotional support helps develop leadership skills in your children, and it is important to include the one that will feel most left out, your ODD youngster.

Then, if you are co-parenting a family with more than one sibling, you know that there's lots of variety when it comes to personality, and this also comes down to there being differences. Something that causes problems between partners is differences, but this is such an important concept to teach to your kids, especially if one of them is so much different from the others. Each of them should understand that, no matter what their differences are, you are a family and you are a team. And because of this and the love and respect you have for each other as family members, you also respect each other's differences.

Finally, working as a team means that there needs to be a mutual understanding of accountability and the acknowledgment of consequences for certain actions. Even though you have a child that is different, it is important that all members of the family are subject to the same rules and that all face the same consequences for breaking rules. Link this concept to the 3 P's to find a system that is uplifting and educational for the whole family (Benjamin, 2020).

Chapter 3: ODD Treatment

ODD, like other mental and mood disorders are treatable, and there is such a wide variety of treatments one can choose from that you may not know where to start. Additionally, applying the "let's start at one point and go through all of them until we find one that works" approach can cause more harm than good, not only to your child or teen's mental state or condition but also to their self-esteem. Imagine jumping from treatment to treatment and being put under the impression that none of them are working on you? That would make me even more discontent and angry at the world, and it can give an ODD child or teen the opportunity to legitimize a reason to act the way they do. There will be a trial and error component with all mental health treatments, but what you want to achieve is minimizing it to the extreme by firstly being informed and secondly, arming yourself with the most current knowledge available. Now that we've covered the nature, symptoms, manifestation, and co-ordinating disorders related to ODD, let's move on to the available treatments, what each type of treatment can offer your child or teen, how they are different and how they may be similar, and the reasons one would opt for a specific type of treatment in specific circumstances.

Why isn't ODD Curable?

Treatment can help you and your child manage oppositional defiant disorder, but there is currently no known cure for it. The reason why medical specialists don't know what the cure is or why it is not curable may be related to the fact that they are not completely sure and can't pinpoint an exact cause. The cause for ODD appears to consist of multiple factors, which include environmental, neurological, and even genetic components. Similar to the fact that researchers and medical practitioners know what the influential and contributing factors are that one can associate with an individual's potential to develop ODD, so are they also aware of therapeutic and psychiatric treatments that can subdue the symptoms, but not cure it completely. The types of treatment for ODD are mostly psychological and in the form of psychotherapy, and some can be applied on their own while others can be used in conjunction with other treatments. Your child's treatment may also depend on whether they have a co-occurring condition, which may affect the approach or techniques required for effective treatment. Below is a discussion of the most common types of ODD treatment and how they work.

Types of ODD Treatment

If you are a parent with an ODD child or teen and you are currently looking for some type of treatment, rest assured that there are many different ways and methods to treat ODD. Speaking to a therapist and giving them the opportunity to get to know your child may also allow them to identify a type of treatment that will work best, which is better than randomly choosing one.

Cognitive Behavioral Therapy

Cognitive behavioral theory, also known as CBT, is characterized as a psychotherapeutic treatment that aims to help people learn how to first identify and then change disturbing or destructive patterns of thought that influence their behavior and emotions negatively. This means that cognitive behavioral therapy aims to change negative thoughts that occur automatically and that cause and can worsen emotional issues in a person's life, which can also be related to depression and anxiety. Studies have indicated that spontaneous negative and even harmful thoughts have a pernicious and unwanted influence on an individual's mood.

The most basic way to explain the CBT process is by identifying three steps during the therapy. First, the negative or harmful thoughts are identified, next, they are challenged by the individual who experienced them with the support of a therapist, and finally, they are to be replaced with thoughts that are more realistic and objective.

The idea behind or the philosophy of CBT is based on the identification of thought patterns. There is quite a wide range of strategies that are used in CBT to help individuals change their thought patterns. These may include role-playing, mental distractions, relaxation techniques, or journaling. Additionally, apart from the fact that there is a variety of techniques, there are also types of cognitive behavioral therapy that are important to be cognizant about. These 'types' are also directly related to the way they differ methodically, although still based on the same philosophy or principles. All the types involve relevant techniques that are aimed at addressing emotions, thoughts, and their subsequent behaviors, and each has a specific focus related to their difference in methodology.

As we mentioned, *Cognitive therapy* is based on identifying and altering distorted or unrealistic thinking patterns, which lead to related emotional responses and subsequent behaviors.

Dialectical behavior therapy or (DBT) also aims to address thoughts and their subsequent emotions and behaviors. However, it utilizes strategies that include mindfulness and emotional regulation.

Multimodal Therapy is a psychological method that requires one to address seven interconnected modalities when addressing thoughts and behavioral issues. These modalities are sensation, behavior, affect, imagery, cognition, interpersonal factors, and biological or drug considerations.

Rational emotive behavior therapy or REBT follows the process of first identifying irrational beliefs, actively challenging the beliefs identified, and then moving to a state of recognition and change to improve thought patterns.

After reading through all the types of CBT, one can see that, although they may take different methodical and therapeutic avenues, the goal remains the same. The nice thing about different types is that a specific approach or therapy type may be more compatible with a certain type of person than another. Although two different individuals may have the same disorder, there are more customized ways to approach and treat them.

CBT is usually used as a short-term treatment but has an astonishingly wide range of disorders that can effectively treat and improve the symptoms. The reason may be because all of these disorders are based on negative or irrational thought patterns. Examples of conditions that benefit from CBT are personality disorders, panic attacks, anxiety disorders, bipolar disorder, addictive behavior, anger problems, phobias, and stress control issues. During CBT, the therapist takes on an active role in the therapeutic process and works hand-in-hand with the patient as opposed to sitting back and only listening. CBT is designed to be a goal-oriented therapy where patients work with their therapists to achieve mutually determined goals. The individual is not kept in the dark about what CBT entails and is aware of all aspects of the therapeutic process.

The impact that CBT aims to make lies in the idea that thoughts and feelings play an underlying and fundamental role in one's behavior. For example, an individual who constantly thinks about car crashes, searches for information about car accidents online and visualizes these incidents will most likely develop a fear for driving and avoid even taking a ride in a car. However, such an individual is not always aware that they have these thought patterns that border on obsession and even more so, that they cause certain negative or unrealistic reactions or behavior. This is where the effectiveness of CBT comes in. By firstly helping an individual to become aware of these persistent and influential thoughts paves the way to the next step, which is engaging with them and understanding them. For a child or teen with ODD, this process may be difficult, especially if they are still young, so the process of explaining it to them is crucial. The pros of CBT is that it has been empirically tested to work on individuals who demonstrate toxic behaviors, and it is usually a more affordable treatment option. Here are the CBT steps that lead to successful change and also two situations that can slow down or negatively impact the progress of CBT:

First, as we've discussed prior, is the identification of negative thoughts. First, the individual must understand how powerful their thoughts are and how their thoughts influence their emotions and behavior. If the individual who is undergoing CBT specifically struggles with introspection, they may need extra assistance as this is a key component to the identification of toxic thoughts and a new process of self-discovery.

Next, new skills that complement and enforce positive behavior need to be identified and implemented. The individual undergoing therapy will ultimately have to practice these skills in real-life situations that will start as a rehearsal process and eventually create a new neural pathway that will cause a natural tendency toward the coping mechanisms and healthy behavior.

Along with the implementation of these new skills and coping mechanisms comes the setting of goals. Without setting goals, these positive reinforcement behaviors will move forward but have no destination.

It is also a crucial component of CBT to focus on the development of problem-solving skills. Problem-solving is part of critical thinking, and this skill will benefit your child even from a young age. Although they will not be able to identify all problems as objectivity is hard as a youngster, you can, with the support of the therapist, help them to systematically develop this life-changing skill. Teenagers will not have such a hard time developing problem-solving skills, although they may need a nudge in the right direction.

After taking all of this in, keep in mind that this transformation is going to be a gradual, if not slow, process. Rushing your child or teen to mentally transform may have the opposite effect, and you can, instead, give them a reason to work hard toward reaching their goal. Tell them how much you love them.

Parent-Child Interaction Therapy

Parent-child interaction therapy, or PCIT, is a combination of behavioral therapy and play therapy that works well for younger children and their caregivers or parents. During this therapeutic process, the adult learns novel skills and techniques that can improve the way they cope with children who have behavioral problems or disorders, emotional issues, language disorders, mental health issues, or language issues. This type of therapy focuses more on the adult to teach and empower them towards developing coping mechanisms and improving their communication with a troubled child, which can involve physical and verbal exchanges.

PCIT is developed for a specific age range, which is from 2 years to 7 years, and if you compare it to the description of cognitive behavioral theory we discussed prior, as a parent, you'll immediately be able to recognize why this may be one of the more appropriate choices for younger children. For example, CBT focuses on the patient and allows them to go through an introspective process that a youngster of 2-3 years will not be able to understand. With PCIT, on the other hand, the control is given to the parents, and they are trained in changing possible triggering behavior and interaction with their young children.

During the PCIT process, parents play with their children in one room while the therapist observes and subsequently coaches the parents from an adjacent room separated by a one-way mirror. During the play process, the therapist and parent communicate using an earphone device to ensure that the parent's responses are specifically tailored to the behavior the child shows during that activity. This also creates a very effective learning process, which would have been based on trial-and-error, but here this element is not significantly reduced due to the observations and leadership of the therapist. Some of the advice a therapist would typically provide a parent is to steer clear of negative language and to ignore negative behavior if it is otherwise harmless. To counter this aspect, they are encouraged to praise for any positive behaviors and show their enthusiasm in these cases. Other skills include reflecting the child's language back to them, which helps them with communication, improving the child's vocabulary by describing the child's activities clearly and audibly and imitating their good behavior to show approval.

PCIT is, in many ways, a relationship-building process taking place in a controlled environment where parents, who take the lead in this process, have the ability to acquire new skills while practicing relationship-building. Improving the relationship you have with your troubled young child can lead to improved behavior, and this can improve family dynamics overall. Long-term practice of this therapy has shown increased confidence in the child, a reduced level of anger, resentment, and aggression, and it ultimately regulates healthy interaction between the parent and the child.

If you recognize any benefits in this description of parent-child interaction therapy that you think may benefit your situation, specifically related to the age of your child, you can locate a qualified therapist by looking for a licensed mental health service provider that holds a master's degree or higher, and that preferably has undergone additional training in PCIT. Additionally, it is imperative that you and your child are able to bond with the therapist and that a trust relationship can be formed (Psychology Today, 2020).

Group Psychotherapy

Group psychotherapy usually involves one or sometimes more than one therapist that works with a group of patients. This type of therapy can be used on its own but is also commonly used in tandem with other types of individual therapy and psychiatric treatment. Groups can start small, meaning it can consist of three to five individuals, but larger groups of up to twelve individuals can also work, especially if the patients bond well. A psychotherapy group would typically meet twice a week, and a session can last one to two hours. Group therapy sessions can be either open or closed, which means that, in some cases, new members are allowed to join during the course of the therapy period. In other cases, patients sign up before the sessions start, and the group membership remains the same.

A typical session for children may include musical therapy, art therapy, and play therapy. The way the sessions are conducted depends on the goal the therapists want to achieve and the condition of the patients. Group psychotherapy for teenagers may involve more talking, sharing of experiences, but expressive activities like art and musical therapy will not be excluded as options due to their therapeutic effects. Therapists have a lot of freedom as to how they want sessions to be conducted, and some sessions can be structured while others can be more spontaneous and free-form.

Group Psychotherapy is used for a myriad of mental conditions and disorders, but it always strives to have the same benefits for its members. One benefit of this type of therapy can offer your child or teen is that they will be among peers as well as the supervision of therapists. While therapists set the breeding ground for positive interaction, the group members can offer support and encouragement by seeing that their fellow members possibly have the same issues and struggles. This can help them to feel less isolated than, for example, at home, where they are the only person experiencing these emotions and outbursts. This leads us to the next pro of group psychotherapy, which is that it gives your child or teen a safe space where they may feel they can say or express things that they cannot do in front of you, at school, or at home. Don't take this personally as it usually means that they may have some toxic feelings they want to get rid of that they don't want to expose you to, and if they are provided an open and safe environment to do so, getting rid of these pent-up emotions can be done is a much healthier way. What happens in the group stays in the group. And, what's especially relevant for children or teens with ODD, in a group setting, the therapist can pay close attention to how they interact with others and how they behave in a social setting, which is usually a problematic situation for children and teens with ODD. Therapists can monitor their behavior and provide valuable feedback.

Finally, another plus is that group therapy is normally a more affordable option like cognitive behavioral therapy, which can have a major role-playing effect in some households (Cherry, 2009).

Applied Behavior Analysis

Applied behavior analysis is one of the treatment options that are often used for aggressive behavior and a lack of impulse control. These are not specifically disorders in themselves, but they are present in, for example, Autism spectrum disorder, conduct disorder, oppositional defiant disorder, and intermittent explosive disorder, most of which are co-operational disorders and which includes our focal point, ODD.

Impulsive and aggressive behavior is often seen as behaviors that reinforce themselves in different social contexts because they have the ability to provoke an instant reaction from their target. This is because, if aggression or impulsive behavior is focused on you, your immediate reaction will be to address it immediately, which means that you gave the person projecting that behavior the attention they wanted. And, of course, your natural reaction to aggressiveness or impulsivity aimed at you will be negative and defensive, which only fuels that reinforcement even more. This is one of the reasons why it is so difficult to change aggressive and impulsive behaviors in children and teens, and applied behavior analysis specifically focuses on analyzing and constructively approaching these behaviors, tackling them proactively.

An applied behavioral therapist or ABA therapist will generally follow a procedure with their patients if the behavioral issue has not been established. They will start by determining which behavior needs attention and requires change and then set goals or identify outcomes that are expected from the therapeutic process. Further, the ABA therapist will, according to the individual situation, decide which measures and techniques they will apply and also establish ways to measure progress and changes in a patient's behavior. Furthermore, the ABA therapist may teach the patient new skills or coping mechanisms, review progress, and ultimately decide whether further behavior modification is necessary in a specific case. As each case is unique, the duration of the therapy is dependent on the severity of the issue and the rate of improvement shown by the patient.

When it comes to treating aggression and impulse control through applied behavior analysis, ABA trained therapists are aware of the attention-related payoff that children and teens with relevant disorders get from these behaviors, so they are trained to show no external reactions toward overt aggressive behavior directed at them. They also train caregivers and parents to do the same. For example, an ABA therapist will advise you to offer a response called neutral redirection as an alternative to punitive measures when being confronted with aggressive behavior.

Neutral redirection is specifically part of applied behavior analysis treating aggression and impulse control-related disorders, and it focuses on empowering the caregiver or authoritative figure to handle the disruptive and aggressive behavior in such a way that it will be eventually subdued. In extreme cases where a child with conduct disorder was to hit a caregiver, they are trained to not show any reaction—not even the slightest flinch. By doing this, they completely dismantle the child's attempt at getting the desired reaction. Neutral redirection teaches the parent, teacher, or caregiver to avoid any reaction and eye contact with the child or teen, which essentially sends the message that they refuse to acknowledge the aggressive or impulsive behavior. When being aggressively attacked, their only response should be to stay calm and guide the aggressive child or teen towards engaging in a more socially acceptable way. Then, only when the child or teen starts behaving in the way they are instructed to by the caregiver will they receive attention and direct acknowledgment. Sounds hard, doesn't it? Trying to adjust to indicating no acknowledgment or reaction whatsoever while being aggressively harassed or insulted by a child requires an immense amount of self-control.

However, looking at ABA and its approach from a more general perspective as it is used for more types conditions than just aggression and impulsivity-related ones, it is important for an ABA therapist to understand how individuals learn certain human behaviors and, based on this principle, how it can be changed or altered over the course of time. The therapist starts by evaluating the child's or teen's behavior and develops a treatment plan based thereon to improve communication and behavioral aspects that need alteration for the child or teen's optimal functioning and development into adulthood. As demonstrated above, one of the pros of ABA therapy is that the therapist can train the caregiver, teacher, and adult. However, for this type of therapy to be effective, continuous evaluation and considerable measures should be taken for effective patient monitoring. As progression starts to show, treatment is modified to fit and promote further progression.

If you are looking for a qualified and able ABA therapist, their practice requirements include graduate-level to a doctorate-level degree; they need to be licensed as a clinical therapist and have additional training and experience in ABA (Psychology Today, 2016; AppliedBehaviorAnalysisEdu.org, 2020).

Family Therapy

Family therapy is classified as a specific type of psychotherapy that traditionally requires the involvement of all members of a nuclear family or a stepfamily, and in some cases, it can also involve members of the extended family depending on their relevance to the situation. The family members attend sessions together that are conducted by either one therapist or a team of therapists who aim to help the family deal or work through issues that are causing dysfunctionalities in the family dynamics and home environment.

The purpose of family therapy is specifically to improve family dynamics, even if there is only one member in the family who has a problem or suffers from an illness. Some of the reasons families attend therapy sessions together is because of the loss of a family member, a mental or physical illness, or issues involving children or teens like ODD. In a case like this or any other case where family therapy is used to deal with the disorder of a child or teen, the purpose is mostly to work through what causes the family's inability to function normally and, similarly, when a new stepfamily has come together and new family dynamics are in the process of forming. At the beginning of the 21st century, therapists started applying a new approach called multisystemic therapy or MST, which is most often done at the family's home so the therapist can experience the ecological environment of the family they are treating. MST is thus often called the "family-ecological systems approach" because a therapist looks at how a family interacts within their home environment. This approach is used, especially when there is a problem child or teen with behavioral issues or emotional disturbances. Several clinical research studies have been conducted on MST, and the general consensus is that it improves family relations, it can decrease adolescent substance use and psychiatric symptoms, and it can improve school attendance.

Family therapy can be conducted by counselors, therapists, social workers, or psychiatrists and involve multiple sessions over an extended period of time. For example, a session would mostly last one hour, and these sessions can occur once a week for three or four months. Here are some interesting concepts related to family therapy, specifically:

The Identified Patient: The identified patient or IP is the individual in the family that is the reason for the family attending family therapy. This makes it sound like we're placing the blame on the IP, but we're simply stating that because of this individual experiencing specific issues or being diagnosed with a specific disorder like ODD, this type of therapy is required and thus attended.

Homeostasis: Homeostasis is a Greek word that means 'balance,' and this word refers to the situation or goal the family seeks to achieve through family therapy. The family wants to restore or work on any situations or causal factors that are causing an imbalance in family dynamics, and thereby reinstate homeostasis or harmonious family life and relationships.

The Extended Family Field: This term is used to describe the immediate family, the network of grandparents, and also includes other family members. In other words, not only the nuclear family. The extended family field is also a term used to refer to and identify what is called an intergenerational transmission of behaviors, problems, and attitudes or emotions. Including members of the extended family, the field can benefit family therapy that is specifically centered around a child or teen.

Differentiation: This term describes each individual family member's ability to be their own person but, at the same time, be able to integrate into a familial community and be part of a greater whole, which is the family. Thus, a healthy family is one that allows differentiation among its members and accepts them as individuals.

Triangular Relationships: This is an interesting family relationship theory that is also often observed in family therapy. The theory says that, when a troubled situation develops between two family members, they are likely to draw in a third member to stabilize the situation and to maintain homeostasis. Some examples of a typical triangular relationship are two parents and a child, a parent, a child, and a grandparent, three children, or two children and a parent. These triangles occur as a natural way to maintain homeostasis in a family setting.

For effective family therapy, a family therapist will first schedule appointments with family members to conduct a series of interviews. These interviews always include all members of the nuclear or stepfamily, but other members can also be interviewed for relevance purposes. For example, if there is an extended family member with a psychiatric illness, the therapist may want to interview this individual, which can help them understand if there are other indirect contributing factors. The interviews allow each family member to provide their version of the issue, and the therapist can get a first impression from each member individually and how they contribute to the functioning of the family before the group sessions start. Things therapists look for in these interviews include the type and levels of emotions expressed by the individual, signs of dominance or submission, the role played by every member in the family, how different members communicate, and whether there are any obvious relationship triangles. The therapist then draws a genogram as part of the preparation process. A genogram is a type of diagram that shows significant events and persons in the family's history and can contain medical history and information of major personality traits. With a genogram, the therapist is able to identify behavioral patterns that stretch over more than one generation, typical marriage choices, possible family secrets, family alliances and previous situations of conflict, and any other details that may be useful for the specific family the therapist is focusing on.

As a final thought regarding family therapy, as effective as it may be on its own and in conjunction with other types of therapy, there are situations in which one needs to take precautions and think about whether the nature of this therapy is suitable for the situation you are experiencing. Examples include families where one or both parents suffer from mental illnesses that include psychosis, antisocial tendencies, or paranoia. Another example is if a family's inherent cultural or religious values do not recognize psychotherapy or harbors suspicions of its practices. A more common example would be a family that is not physically able to meet regularly enough for effective therapy to be conducted. It's always best to look at the pros and cons, but family therapy, and especially MST is a great option for children and teens with ODD that causes disruption in a household (Encyclopedia of Children's Health, 2020).

Psychological Counseling for Children and Adolescents

A child psychologist is specifically trained to help a child understand themselves from their own perspective. In other words, if a child has a disorder or a mental illness, the psychologist will help them to figure out what's going on in their minds by using their way of thinking and reasoning as a starting point. Child counseling focuses on children, adolescents and teens that battle with mental disorders or mental illness. Additionally, this type of counseling is used to help children who are experiencing trauma or high levels of grief or who live in a dysfunctional environment at home. The goal of child counseling is to break down stressful situations, and problems children experience to make them seem more approachable and, ultimately, conquerable. If your child is someone who is trained to see things and communicate things to them from their level and perspective, then child counseling can greatly benefit your child or teenager.

Because child counselors are trained to communicate with your child or teenager on their level instead of trying to lift them to your level, the child may bond more easily with the counselor, a trust relationship can be established quicker, and your child is likely to tell the counselor things about their life and their feelings that are important and relevant to their condition, but that they would never have revealed under other circumstances.

Child counselors are trained to treat a wide variety of issues that children and teenagers experience. These issues include disorders and mental illness, but also expand to grief and trauma like divorce, relocation, and the death of a loved one, bullying, sexual or emotional abuse, and family-related addiction or substance abuse. They also tend to use methods like cognitive behavioral therapy if they think it is the best way to treat a child's condition, but their approach would differ slightly because of their specialized training. From a child counselor's perspective, there are specific behavioral signs that can be an indicator that your child or teen can benefit from child counseling. These include the leakage of urine, unprovoked aggression, if the child has significant difficulty adjusting to new situations like a social situation, issues with academic performance, if your child experiences constant and excessive anxiety, a sudden disinterest in previous hobbies and activities, addiction or drug abuse, self-harm, or hearing voices.

If you feel that your child needs this specific approach, then you can try a child counselor to see if your child benefits from this specialized method of communication (Langham, 2019).

Psychiatry

Drug treatment for ODD is not deemed as the first best option as there are no FDA-approved medications for oppositional defiant disorder in the United States. This being said, there are specific drugs that can perform a "rewiring" process in the brain and improve the symptoms of ODD in children and adolescents. Children diagnosed with ODD have shown signs of improved behavior when administered low doses of atypical neuroleptics like Abilify (aripiprazole) and Risperdal (risperidone). Medication should, however, not be considered a primary option due to the absence of approved medicative substances (Rodden, 2017).

Homeopathy

There are individuals who believe that ODD can be treated with homeopathic remedies, and there are many individuals who are opposed to psychiatric medicine due to its many side-effects. Homeopathy is used for ODD, but is a lesser-known treatment option. Let's look at what homeopathy entails and how homeopathic treatments can work for your ODD child or teen and which ones are recommended.

Homeopathy is classified as a medical science which, in its diagnostic process, considers the physiological and psychological components of an individual in relation to how the disease in question has evolved in the body or mind. This concept is used and all these factors are considered when prescribing a homeopathic remedy. A homeopath believes that, using this method, they are more likely to find the root cause of an illness or a disorder as a medical doctor only looks at the physical and a psychiatrist focuses on pharmaceutical drugs, while their remedies remain natural. Considering these details, it is safe to say that homeopathy has a holistic methodology.

When consulting a homeopath, they will take down a record of your physical ailments, including undiagnosed complaints, physical and psychological attributes, and the emotional situation you are in during the consultation. This approach makes it easier for the practitioner to find the root cause of an issue by looking at it through a holistic lens, and it gives the patient the opportunity to rid themselves of any thoughts that have been bothering them, as these thoughts will also be deemed important by the homeopath.

As opposed to psychiatric medicine, homeopathic remedies are deemed to be safe, they have no side-effects, and they are in their natural form. Homeopathic remedies are also known to improve the immune system and renew energy levels. Homeopathic medicine aims to balance the psychological, biological, and emotional issues or disturbances a child experiences when they have ODD and subsequently improves the child's behavior. Homeopathic medicine also claims to prevent an ODD child from experiencing a relapse, which would be a recurrent episode that happens after the child started the treatment. By using homeopathic medicine, the child's mind, which is in distress, can be stabilized and positive behavior can start developing. An interesting trait of homeopathic medicine is that it is patient-oriented, which means that the medicine prescribed is based on the characteristics of the patient instead of solely on the symptoms of the condition. As you will see, the recommended medicines include characteristics that are not part of ODD's usual symptoms. Here are three examples:

- *CINA:* This remedy is especially effective for children who are irritable, anxious, and restless. The child can also be described as petulant, dissatisfied, and angry, and dislikes to be touched. The child is very demanding but will not accept anything that is offered to him. These children also tend to be overweight and have a large appetite.
- *NATRUM MURIATICUM:* Treatment for children who are irritable, easily offended, impulsive, and can be abusive towards others. This remedy can also help if a child is malnourished or needs vitamins.
- *ANTIMONIUM CRUDUM:* This remedy is specifically for children who have excessive anger and act in an abusive way towards others. The child is moody, will often ignore someone who speaks to them, and can easily become irritated.

They seem to get angry for no reason and they crave attention (Welcome Cure, 2020).

As you can see, these remedies are extremely specific and sometimes contain strange information about the person it's treatment is aimed at. However, there are more than 50 different remedies used to treat Oppositional Defiant Disorder in homeopathy, whereas in psychiatric medicine there are two. The question is, will your child fit the profile of one of those fifty remedies? It is an interesting methodology, and the experience may be therapeutic for the soul.

ODD Home Care

One of the most difficult challenges of living with an ODD child or teen is to separate their violent and disruptive behavior from who they are as a person. Because, they are not their disorder. They are children/young adults that require direction and affection. Because you usually associate people with the way they behave, to suddenly not do it is incredibly difficult, especially if it is your own flesh and blood. Here are a few tips that can help you to manage and stabilize an otherwise stormy household.

Firstly, don't react to or engage in a power struggle with your child or teen. If you are an ODD mom, you know that this is something they instigate often, and you can dismantle the potential conflict situation just as quickly by not going for the bait. Another way to keep a steady boat is to choose which battles you want to fight and which you'll leave. For example, there will be lots of provocation and opportunistic attempts at conflict, but some will be more serious than others. Do you have to react to a provocation if it's not that serious? The idea of not reacting doesn't mean you should always ignore your child, but you can respond in a non-confrontational way which shows them that you are willing to pay attention, but you are not available for fighting about willy-nilly stuff.

Then, you know they're going to break them, but it's imperative to establish and uphold clear rules in the household and make it clear that it is unacceptable when a rule is broken. An ODD child or teen is going to use this structure to rebel against, but without a clear household structure, you are not providing the child with a good example of how to live their life. This being said, you should also provide your child with the opportunity to express themselves in the form of innocent play. These are moments of healthy expression, so enjoy them with your child or teen if you can.

Try not to bombard your child or teen with too many questions, even if you have some burning ones. If they look like they want to talk, then they are showing you a need to talk, but you have this handy little guide for any general information about ODD you may need. Don't depend on or expect your child to explain the disorder to you as this can be burdensome for them.

Help your child to follow a routine as this structure can be something they can lean on when things don't go well. This may sound strange as ODD children and teens seem to want to destroy routine and authority, but you can find a way to suggest it to them that will have them slip into it without them even noticing. Routine for someone with a mental or mood disorder can be like a walking frame when every limb in their body feels like it doesn't want to move. Finding a way to introduce a sense of routine without appearing authoritative, which can spark a reaction or an episode, is the trick (Mauro, 2019).

Chapter 4:

A Healthy Lifestyle for ODD

Children and Teens

Mental and physical health are closely interlinked and one should never underestimate the power of a healthy lifestyle. However, can dietary requirements help children with behavioral issues like ODD or is this just a myth? Considering how many other disorders there are that's associated with ODD, and can be co-occurring, teaching your child to follow a healthy lifestyle is definitely not a bad idea. There are also specific nutrients that one can focus on to improve the brain's ability to function and your child's overall mood that is worth mentioning. And, why not incorporate some healthy movement into their hobbies and activities? This chapter takes a look at how to best approach nutrition and physical health for your ODD child and teen, and it will also provide some great family-time ideas with a happy ending in mind.

Dietary Requirements – Are There Any?

Although a medical practitioner will most likely refer you to a therapist or in a more serious scenario prescribe medication, claims of taking specific nutrients in the form of supplements have surfaced in discussions and articles. In these articles, writers claim that the use of specific nutrients is effective and worth trying if your child is struggling with severe ODD symptoms. Nutrients are present in food, and they are also available in supplement form. The discussion below will focus on when you should consider a supplement and how you can look for nutrient-rich foods that provide the good stuff in the most natural way possible.

Omega 3 Fatty Acids

Omega 3 is an all-around miracle worker, and ADHD patients are known to take a concentrated form of Omega 3 to help with their symptoms. This is because this fatty acid, that the body cannot create itself, is a crucial nutrient for the maintenance and, in the case of children, the development of the brain. Omega 3 fatty acids don't only help for ADHD, it has a myriad of pros when it comes to ailments concerning brain function that affects young and old alike. It is also considered to be a crucial nutrient required by humans, but it is not available in a wide range of foods. This is why many people choose to take an Omega 3 supplement to make up for its deficit in our modern diet. Omega 3 contains two types of fatty acids called DHA and EPA. Both are vital for optimal brain function and development from childhood, but EPA is especially therapeutic when it comes to mental health issues. To use Omega 3 for therapeutic measures such as treating symptoms of ADHD or ODD, look for a specific fish oil or supplement that has a higher EPA than DHA ratio. The recommended ratio is at least twice the amount of EPA than DHA.

One of the issues Omega 3 fatty acids have been studied to relieve and improve is anxiety. A study conducted at the China Medical University Hospital, where subjects were compared by either being administered Omega 3 polyunsaturated fats or placebo's, provided a surprising result as patients who were administered the Omega 3 indicated significant decreases in their anxiety levels. Anxiety is a component that is prevalent not only in ODD but in most of its co-occurring conditions. Apart from this, considering that your child's brain will be growing throughout childhood and adolescence and that Omega 3 fatty acids are crucial for neural development apart from having these benefits for children and teens that have ODD, it seems almost strange that there is not a community van driving around in the streets bellowing, "Remember to give your children their daily dose of Omega 3 fatty acids" through a crackling megaphone (Demko, 2018).

What would we do without good ol' Omega 3?

Don't Forget about Vitamin E!

This is true. We can't forget about Vitamin E because it helps absorb the Omega 3! That's the most important reason. However, since we're here, let's take a look and see if Vitamin E has any other benefits of note.

Vitamin E appears to have many benefits and important functions that include improved vision, healthy blood, healthy skin, and a healthy brain. Vitamin E is also a rich source of antioxidants, which protects human cells against the damage of free radicals. The good news about Vitamin E is that it's not as scarce in our everyday diet as Omega 3 fatty acids are. You can get your Vitamin E by consuming peanuts, olive oil, canola oil, almonds, or even meat and dairy products. So, even though Vitamin E helps you get the best from your superpowered Omega 3, it also has its own benefits. And, for a child, it is not necessary to provide a supplement if you give them a good old peanut butter sandwich on a regular basis (Mayo Clinic Staff, 2020).

Zinc

Zinc has a really interesting benefit. While studies were conducted on children with ADHD, researchers found that they had lower levels of zinc than children who don't have ADHD, and hypothesized that there may be a possible link. Today, we know that zinc can have a therapeutic effect for children and teens who have ODD as it can decrease levels of impulsivity, hyperactivity, but strangely enough, not any aspect related to inattentiveness. It is also important to note that zinc is known as an essential nutrient just like Omega 3 fatty acids, which means that the human body doesn't produce this nutrient. If your child or teen with ODD displays any of these two symptoms, which is not only common in ODD but also in co-occurring conditions, you can visit your doctor and ask that a check is done on your child's zinc levels. This may solve a problem that you previously didn't know how to solve and that didn't show results under therapy alone. Zinc levels that are too low can be problematic, but so can levels that are too high. So, if you are considering giving your child an extra supplement, the best decision is to first consult your doctor.

Magnesium

Magnesium is one of the most abundant minerals in the body, and most people are not aware of the multiple functions it has in ensuring physical and mental health. That being said, Magnesium is also not as prevalent in our modern diet of processed and flavored foods as it used to be, so many people have a magnesium deficiency without them knowing it. A study in 2017 reviewed 18 previous studies conducted on magnesium and the researchers concluded that magnesium does, in fact, have a therapeutic effect on anxiety. This is because magnesium works with our muscles, our brain, and our nervous system and it regulates a part of the brain called the hypothalamus. The hypothalamus regulates two glands in your brain called the pituitary and the adrenal glands, and these glands are responsible for regulating your anxiety levels. Apart from anxiety, there are other great reasons for one to focus on maintaining healthy magnesium levels. For example, it helps with muscular pain and relaxation, it can give you a great night's sleep, it improves your mood, keeps your blood pressure normal, and it can be used to treat migraines.

If you want to first try to improve your child's magnesium intake through their diet, then there are foods you can incorporate that are high in magnesium. These foods include leafy greens like kale and spinach, avocado, legumes, dark chocolate, nuts and seeds, and sticking to whole grains. If you want to look for ways to reduce stress and anxiety naturally, you can try pushing up the magnesium intake in your child's diet or consult a doctor about a supplement. Magnesium truly is a super mineral (Ferguson, 2019; Additude, 2016).

Apart from focusing on these helpful nutrients, it is important to understand the dangers of the high-sugar, processed food diet if your child has a mental or behavioral disorder. Sugar wreaks havoc in a child's system who struggles with their mood, behavior, hyperactivity, and when eating only refined carbohydrates, one can hardly expect to get any of that zinc from the snowy white hamburger bun you just gave them to eradicate. Following an 80% whole foods and a 20% what-kids-love-to-eat foods approach can help to balance out nutritional issues you were not aware of, which can lead to behavioral improvement.

The 80/20 Principle

Children don't want to be on a constant health journey, so the 80/20 principle is a great way to treat them every now and then if you are focused on giving them a nutritious eating plan. The 80/20 principle means that you eat well 80% of the time and you treat yourself 20% of the time. It's just the right ratio to stay healthy and satisfied. If you were to put this in practice, it would mean that the kids can have a small-to-medium sized candy bar one or two times a week, and on Friday night the family can have pizza and ice cream. The rest of the week will be spent eating nutrient-rich foods. If you think my 20% is a little sparse, which it maybe is, you can up the treats a tiny bit. It's important for your children to enjoy healthy food as well as their treats, and if your kids are still young, you've got the ball in your hands. Little ones are easy to teach good eating habits because habits are difficult to change when a child gets older. So, if your child is used to more junk food, they are going to give you a very hard time if you try to implement the 80/20. But, don't let that faze you. Nutritious foods can also taste good; once you get them off the preservatives and salt and they get their taste buds back, they'll be more compliant. Have some fun with the 80/20 by asking your kids what they want as treats each week. Just make sure they understand the relative size the treat's supposed to be, and you'll end up with a satisfied bunch. If you are looking for some information about clean eating and whole foods, you can read about the clean eating philosophy and how you can magically turn some junk food favorites into whole food options by reading right below.

The Whole Foods and Clean Eating Philosophy

What do all of these phrases mean? Is clean eating what you do and whole foods what you do it to? Or are they basically the same concept? I think I may be confusing everyone, including myself, so let's start again:

"Whole foods" is a term that is usually applied to foods like fruits, vegetables, whole grains, and legumes that have undergone minimal to no processing. However, animal products can also be classified as "whole foods." The problem comes in when you want to classify foods that are not completely processed but they are also not completely 'whole' anymore. It appears that there are several phases or layers of processing that make very few foods 100% whole- only those you pluck directly from a tree, in fact. This is because even processes like washing and chopping are seen as processing just like canning and preserving foods would be seen as processing. But there's a big difference between just washing a food and canning it; with canned foods, you add preservatives and additives to make it last longer. So, this is where the crux of the distinction lies; not all food processing procedures are equal.

In fact, the phrases "minimally-processed" and "ultra-processed" were invented to help us just in case we become confused. Minimally-processed food refers to food that has undergone processing that left the food close to its natural state. In this case, washing would be a good example; the dirt and pesticides were washed from the food, but there was nothing added to change the composition of the food in itself. This also means that the food maintains most of its original nutritional value if it is only minimally processed. As minimal processing moves to ultra processing, ingredients like salt, sugar, and fat are added that causes a decrease in the food's nutritional value.

This basically means that it's not possible to eat a 100% clean diet, but that eating foods that are minimally processed and that still resembles it's most natural state is the best way to provide the most nutrients you can from food to your family and to children who need to focus on nutrients and nourishment. Here are some examples of how you can make simple whole food swaps from previously processed options:

- Instead of using white bread, swap it for bread that is wholegrain or wholemeal.
- Chuck away the Cheerios and give your child a bowl of steel-cut oats with fresh banana or blueberries.
- Trade in the snack bar for a handful of unsalted, mixed nuts.
- Try to stick to fresh, free-range chicken instead of purchasing protein from the deli section.

- When you visit the grocery store again, opt for fresh fruit instead of buying fruit juice; it contains so much more fiber and provides the correct amount of fructose per serving.

There are other options you can consider too, like swapping your white basmati rice for the brown version, trying to rather make something from scratch than buying the premade version. There's not always enough time for this, but every small step makes a difference. And, teaching your child to love whole foods from a young age will likely cause the habit to stick as they grow older, making them strong and healthy adults. Consider the 80/20 principle, and have some fun in the kitchen. (Health Agenda, 2017).

Productive Activities and Hobbies

When we talk about productive activities and hobbies for children and teens with ODD, what we are actually referring to is activities that will provide extra aid in subduing the aggression and defiance and that will promote a sense of physical and mental relief, decreased anxiety, and an improved mood. Exercise is one of the most widely researched natural aids for depression and anxiety because it is a virtually free alternative to expensive therapy sessions and, in some cases, medication. What research has found regarding exercise, however, is that normal low-intensity movement may keep a healthy person mentally in shape, but when an individual suffers from a condition or a disorder like depression or anxiety, a higher intensity level of exercise is required to get that same benefit. This is most likely due to the brain of a person who has depression or anxiety's inability to produce enough of the required neurotransmitters when doing the same amount of exercise a healthy person would.

The Benefits of Organized Sport

When it comes to the requirements you are looking for for your child or teen's activities and hobbies, one of the best options out there is participating in organized sport. It's almost like a tailor-made treatment program for a child with conduct and behavioral issues. Let's look at the benefits sports offer children in general without considering they may have a disorder like ODD:

Apart from sport being an excellent way to stay active and to exercise on high-intensity and low-intensity levels, there are so many other benefits parents should know about. There are team sports and individuals sports, and each one has its own unique qualities. The trick is to pick the type of sport that is right for your child, which can ultimately help change their attitude, their outlook on life, the way they react towards rules and boundaries, and their overall development as human beings. Let's look at the general benefits of playing sports that are applicable to all children and teens first.

Children, especially those who play sports from a young age and continue to play throughout their childhood, are prone to have well-developed vision, and they are also less likely to develop vision problems. Then, of course, playing sports is one way to keep your child healthy and help them to maintain a healthy weight for their age. Studies indicate that children who are active, specifically those who participate in an activity after school, are more likely to maintain a normal weight. Then, your child will be able to develop and finetune their coordination and motor skills just from learning to play and participating in organized sport. Motor skills and coordination come in handy doesn't matter where you are in your life—even when you're driving a car, and children who have participated in organized sports generally have a very well-developed sense of coordination and good motor skills.

Then, if you find your youngster a sport that fits their dynamics and personality, the sense of team spirit and positive relationships they will develop with teammates and coaches can develop self-identify and boost their self-esteem. It's almost like recreating the family teamwork dynamics at home, and it also has a very rewarding goal for kids when they work together and reach their team's goals. What a priceless quality to learn that can support a child to reach a healthy state of mind as an adult that can ultimately get them far in their life journey.

What's left? Why, fun and friendship! This one may be tricky for your ODD youngster or teen as they are also likely to show disrespect towards their peers. However, if they are able to find friendship in this venture, it will be life-changing for them.

After looking at these pros, which are applicable outcomes for all children who participate in organized sport, how do you choose a sport that's right for your child? Firstly, they need to be into the idea of playing a sport. My young one had an affinity for karate because she thought it was all about fighting. To her surprise, it was not about fighting at all; it was about restraint and respect. Nevertheless, she was willing to make the mental shift as she enjoyed the educational and physical aspects of the sport, so I knew that we had found the right activity for her. After picking her up from a lesson, she would be calmer, more open to suggestion and instruction, and she would sleep better. However, that's not what we're here for. We are here to focus on your child and their health, so let's look at our options.

The first aspect to look at when you are looking at different sports options is what your child or teen is generally interested in. Even better, if your child has an interest in a specific sport, this can make the process easier. On the other hand, being interested or enjoying watching a specific sport doesn't mean you'd want to play that sport, just like some girls like to watch football. So, let's dig a bit deeper.

What do you think is your child's biggest mental or emotional need at this point that can be satisfied through playing a sport? For example, if your child is not a team-sports kind of person, there may not be any sense in looking into these options, and you may find better results looking at options like tennis, squash, track, or another type of sport where your child competes as an individual. Some children enjoy individual sports because the focus shifts from teamwork to developing an inner sense of individual drive that can be great for learning about perseverance and self-belief.

It is also important to only take into account sports that will match the abilities of your child. For example, some children have co-occurring disorders like ADHD or they can even have conditions like asthma that may affect which sports they are compatible with. It's important to inform the coach about your child or teen's conditions, whether they are mental or physical. When you and your child have found a sport they want to try out, put the foundation or sports organization that is responsible for organizing and training through your own assessment process. Ask yourself the following questions regarding the sports club or organization you and your child are looking to join:

Does this program have a vision and a mission that matches your own or are there clashes in your beliefs or views and the ones of the program or organization?

What level of involvement does the organization expect from you as a parent?

Do the practice and game schedules match you and your child's schedules?

How do the coaches select team members? Do you agree with the selection process, and do you think it is fair?

Is there adequate supervision and do the coaches and management team appear to be responsible and experienced?

Is the program well-organized or do they just go with the flow?

Finally, does the program or organization have some sort of insurance that can cover any injuries sustained by your child whilst training or during a game?

If any of these points are of interest or importance to you, I suggest you create a list of selection criteria and use it to choose the best organization or club your child can join. If you live in a smaller area and the setting is more informal but you know most of the people involved, then most of these criteria may not be necessary. You can choose which ones you want to use (Stanford Children's Health, 2019).

Sports have shown to be specifically effective and therapeutic for children and teens who have ADHD. Because ADHD and ODD are so closely related, studying the benefits can also bring some final insight into the physical and mental benefits that have been recorded through research and ongoing studies.

Athletic skills have been called an "island of competence" your child can use to develop a level of resilience and a high self-esteem that can help them deal with their diagnosis. For children who have ADHD, individual sports that are focused on developing and mastering a specific skill is especially beneficial. Examples include martial arts, swimming, archery, ballet, and even diving. This element of focus is great for improving their sense of concentration and focus and the physical aspect helps them to get rid of excess energy. One of the best things about sport for a child that has to deal with the diagnosis of a disorder is the sense of achievement and accomplishment they get from it. There is no equivalent to how valuable this is for the development of their self-worth and self-esteem, which can, in many cases, be the reason they lash out (CHADD, 2018).

Artistic Endeavors

Expressive activities like art can also be very therapeutic for children with ODD. Just like you're expressing yourself physically when playing sports, some children or teens may be more suited to expressing themselves emotionally or artistically. You can talk to your child about attending an extra-curricular art class or you can take them to an art shop and buy some supplies so they can experiment at home. If possible, create them their own little art space where they can practice their creativity. Good options are acrylic paints as they are water-based and quick-drying as opposed to oil paint, which takes forever to dry and is very hard to clean once it messes. You can also buy them a set of drawing pencils, charcoal, a sketch pad, and a canvas or two. They can purchase an ebook that contains tutorials or watch YouTube tutorials on how to create landscapes, seascapes, impressionist paintings, realist images—you name it.

When they've created something that you know they've worked hard on and you know they are proud of, frame it and put it up against the wall where everyone can see it. This act of appreciation will do wonders for their self-esteem.

Writing a Tell-all

I think all children who struggle emotionally and psychiatrically should have a diary. In fact, everyone struggles, so everyone can benefit from having a diary. Some people just enjoy writing more than others, just like some people enjoy painting more than others. Writing is another therapeutic way of getting pent-up energy out of your system–energy that may have been unfairly projected on a family member. Just as you would have bought your child proper art supplies, buy them a nice diary. Buy them one with a cover that they will like; one that they will enjoy opening and writing in every day. And add a special pen. You can even make a pact with them that, every time they feel like acting out, they first have to write down how they are feeling in their diary before acting out. Tell them that the diary belongs to them and that no-one will read it, so they can write whatever they want in it, as long as they write how they feel at that moment.

That diary may look a bit worn down after a few months, but that doesn't matter. When it's full, tell your child to store it in a special place and get them a brand new one.

Positive Reinforcement

While we're on the topic of raising healthy ODD munchkins or larger versions of them, let's look at ways they can be encouraged to develop healthy habits. One way to sneakily work on changing your child or teen's habits is by using behavior modification techniques. I know, it kind of sounds like you'd have to strap your child to a chair and put electrodes all over their forehead and temples and push a big red button. However, the simplicity of the reality may shock you. If you want to modify the behavior of your ODD child or teen, a very effective way to do so is by using positive reinforcement. From an ODD child's perspective, they are usually expecting a scolding, a reprimanding, or a punishment as a response to their destructive behavior. So, if this method doesn't involve strapping them to a chair, or any type of furniture for that matter and it is still effective, how does it work? Positive reinforcement has shown to improve misbehaviors like acting aggressively towards others and violating or breaking rules. It also encourages social-friendly behaviors like following directions and (willingly) sharing with others.

Another reason for applying positive reinforcement is to help your child develop a sense of responsibility by doing their chores, completing their homework, and getting along with other family members without arguing or being difficult about it. Let's take this step-by-step and start by looking at the theory behind the genius.

Would you get up and go to work every day and most likely work late once or twice a week if you didn't get a paycheck at the end of the month? I'm not referring to work for charity organizations here—I'm talking about your average primal 9-5 daily grind most people go through to keep food on the table, minus the occasional feel-good moment when you show your colleague how to plug in their computer. Well, let me tell you, I most certainly won't. What's the point of going through all that sweat, tears and stress if there's no reward or payoff? What's that 'thing' called that keeps us going to work every day? That's basically positive reinforcement. In adult terms, it's another word for remuneration, but how does it translate into ODD child/teen language?

Firstly, like adults, kids are wired the same way; if they receive positive reinforcement for their good behavior, they will maintain this behavior. The same goes for hard work; positive reinforcement will motivate a child to maintain a certain standard in their work if they know that they will be rewarded for it. Here are examples of how you can implement positive reinforcement in very simple ways for smaller children to more sneaky and complicated ways for older children and teens who would want expensive stuff:

- Cheering and clapping will work on the youngsters. A teenager may think it's the most lame and embarrassing thing that's ever happened to them, which I, personally, would find quite amusing.
- A good high-five can go both ways, depending on the context. Try not to high-five your teen in

front of their friends, though. They may, however, value it as a private celebration moment between the two of you.

- Hugging is a great way to reinforce your child because of its affectionate nature. This approach will work very well with youngsters and it will help satisfy their appetite for affection and attention. Sometimes an ODD child will resist this type of affection, but in the context of achievement and approval, it will most likely be a great success.

- Now, here is something you can also apply to your teens. It involves spending some special time together. So, of course your little one would like to go out for an ice cream, but you can also take your teen out for lunch or dinner or coffee. Take the time to say uplifting things to your child and have a laugh. And a slice of cherry pie.

- Why don't you try talking positively about your child, in front of your child, with another adult? For example, "Jenny painted the most beautiful picture of a still life yesterday. Yes, she even arranged and designed the still life herself! I'm getting it framed for the living room." Your child will feel like the most important person in the world!

- In other situations, you can give them tangible rewards or extra privileges—these work well with older children. For example, you can extend your teen's curfew by an hour as a reward for good behavior or compliance with the house rules. Or, you can give your little one some extra TV time or video game time.

Praise

Praise is also a fantastic way to apply positive reinforcement, and there are different ways you can use praise to increase its effectiveness. Kids often act out because, when they actually exhibit any form of good behavior, it sometimes goes unnoticed, which makes them feel that they are doing it in vain. We can't exactly expect a child to do their chores for the sake of the greater good, now can we? The ironic part of all of this is that negative behavior is what gets the most attention from parents, where it should actually be the opposite. If two children were gallivanting around the house but one is jumping on and ruining your new leather couch while the other is just sweetly building a Lego castle, which one will most likely get your attention? I think we'll all start by frantically trying to get the wild one off the couch. The other one, however, also needs to be recognized for their good manners. What if you turned the situation around and focused on praising the good behavior and ignoring the couch-hopping? There would be two children quietly sitting and playing Lego in no time. If you give your child positive feedback on what they are doing, they are likely to act out, and by applying this technique on an ODD child or teen, you may be able to influence their pattern of outbursts to become less frequent and even diminish the triggers that cause them.

Behaviors that are especially responsive to praise are very similar to those that react well to positive reinforcement; this is probably because verbal praise is a form of positive reinforcement. Let's go through behaviors that are specifically responsive to praise:

Firstly, there is prosocial behavior again. If your child or teen is willing to take turns without fighting, use positive or kind words, is willing to share with others, and makes an effort to get along with others in general, these are all actions that respond well to praise, and praising your child in these situations can create a pattern of reinforced behavior. Then, if your child shows any form of compliance, which is usually a rare scenario if you have an ODD child or teen, this behavior reacts successfully to praise. Compliance can include following general rules, following instructions set by an authoritative figure, and even just minding their own business when they could've been participating in naughty and destructive behavior. Finally, an action that should be in the least acknowledged and praised is when your ODD child shows that they are making an effort; even better if they are making an effort to improve in areas that need improvement. Even if they are not quite there yet, praising their efforts will motivate them to keep trying and to stay strong.

Now that we've looked at situations that partner well with praise, it is also important to focus on strategically applying praise to get the maximum effect and reinforcement from it. Funnily enough, if praise is not given appropriately, it can be unhealthy for your child's perception of themselves and their abilities, which can be damaging for them when they enter the world as adults. By looking at the following examples of healthy methods, the unhealthy ones will most likely become clear to you as well.

Firstly, provide realistic praise. We all think that our children are the smartest, most beautiful and most special children on the planet, but telling them this too often may not be too good for them. For example, instead of saying, "Maggie, you are the best ballet dancer I've ever seen," try to identify an actual positive feat that you can encourage and focus on that. For example, change it to "you really did a great job with your pirouettes; I can see that you've been practicing hard!" If the praise is actually applicable to an aspect or technique that your child has been working on, they will feel even more validated and loved because they know that you've been paying attention and that you noticed the improvement.

Linking closely to the above approach, constructive praise includes avoiding labeling your child. Labeling is just a short version of providing exaggerated or non-specific praise. Even if this is your honest opinion and your child may have an IQ of 140+, it's not productive to call him "Mommy's little genius." An old school friend of mine decided to become a medical doctor, and, when her mother refers to her or talks about her, she doesn't call her by her name–she actually talks about "my daughter that's a doctor." Every single time. Which do you think your child would prefer, for their parents to acknowledge them as a person or to identify them by their highly-acclaimed profession? This is an example of how this type of praise can go horribly wrong and actually be bad for your child even though your intentions are to show love and appreciation.

Then, you can get the most out of praising your child by being specific when you praise them. Most of us say "great job" and assume that our children understand what we are referring to. However, enunciation has an effect on how a child interprets praise. You can say "well done" or you can say "well done for remembering to take out the trash!" Personally, I'd appreciate the second one because I know what I'm being praised for.

Now, here's an interesting one that I've come across when socializing with other parents who have children. It's almost as if the concept of praise is not understood completely. A parent would praise their child, but they would include a negative phrase or connotation within the message. It reminds me of how my grandmother approached the concept of praise; I once told her that I got a good score for a test, and she responded by saying, "Well, now you can make it even better next time." Is there actually praise in there somewhere? I never told her anything about my test scores again. From my perspective as a child, the good score was not really acknowledged in the praise, but I realized later in my life that it was implied. However, implied praise is not enough for a child. It is the same with giving praise, which is supposed to be a positive experience and message, but lacing it with negativity or scorn. For example, "I'm proud of you for not trying to ruin dinner." The duality in that sentence will not motivate your child and their focus will immediately fall on the latter part of the sentence, which contains negative wording. Your child's thoughts will most likely be, "Oh, Mom or Dad thinks I always ruin dinner. Great." This can possibly backfire and cause negative reinforcement. Instead, you can try "I'm proud of you for being so positive and chatting with everyone at the dinner table tonight." What's your opinion on this? Have you ever caught yourself giving praise to your child that is laced with negativity? When dealing with an ODD child or teen, your child's repeated misbehavior and aggression can program your brain into a negative copilot mode, and negative words will subsequently leave your mouth spontaneously, even if you want to communicate a positive message. This is completely understandable. So, this specific part of how praise can be effective if used strategically is one that parents with troubled children, like children and teens with ODD, should pay attention to.

Finally, with the focus on children with behavioral disorders, you can superpower your praise and boost their self-esteem by praising their effort and not its outcome. The outcome will not always be successful, but you can always praise your child for making an effort. They will be motivated to step up that effort, and this can eventually lead them to success. How proud can a parent be of a child that keeps on trying, even if they are struggling? They deserve acknowledgment and praise from those who love them most (Morin, 2019).

Organizing Constructive Family Time

When it comes to organizing some family time, there are lots of things you and your family can do, depending on what everyone enjoys doing and focusing on activities that will improve family dynamics and relationships. Here are some goals to consider when looking at different family activities:

Firstly, the activity will be ideal if it fits into your family's team goal or vision. For example, if one of your goals is to improve relationships between the siblings, then setting an activity that promotes this goal is ideal.

Secondly, organizing an activity that everyone will enjoy will also help a lot. Your ODD child and especially your ODD teen may act like there's nothing that interests them, but don't let it faze you. By observing your child's everyday activities, you will definitely have a clear idea of their interests, likes, and dislikes.

Finally, maintain a balance between the type of activities that you'd like your family to partake in. For example, try not to plan all of them to be at home or in front of the TV. Try going outdoors or doing something active, and change the scenery a bit. You know your family–have some fun! Consider these examples as a basis that you can build your own authentic activities on:

A Movie Night with a Twist

How diverse is your family in terms of age? Do you have teens and tweens? Are there some conflicting ideas when it comes to everyone's favorite movie? I know what it's like watching a movie someone else is absolutely crazy about and you just want to fall asleep. However, movie nights can be fun bonding experiences. Well, if you have tiny tweens, move choices are going to be more limited, but otherwise, each family member gets to search Netflix, choose a movie, and you throw all the movie names in a hat. Or a plastic container if you don't have a sturdy hat. Make sure that nobody can see the names by writing them on paper and folding the paper in half, leaving the blank sides showing. Then, schedule a day every week or every second week when the family will come together for movie night—no excuses!

Each night, make one person's favorite snacks (you can create a separate hat containing everyone's preferences and draw one each time if you want) put the mattresses down on the floor in front of the TV to make sure there's space for everyone, and get comfy. You can even decide to wear your pajamas every time you have a movie night. Focus on constructive conversation and make sure that everyone's opinion and comments are treated equally.

Keeping Active

There really is no better way to remind your children about how precious nature is than stuffing them all in the car and taking them on a family hike. If you live near scenic nature reserves or hiking spots, this is a great activity for your family that will also allow everyone to get some exercise. You can incorporate activities like bird-watching, photography, and getting to know the different trees and plants that grow in your area. If there's a lake in the area, go swimming or tanning—your kids will love that. You can play games on the beach and have a picnic.

On the other hand, if you're only going for a hike, you can also have a picnic or you can take everyone out to lunch when it gets too hot to be outside. If it's winter, you can take everyone ice skating—there really is a lot to do outdoors. If you want to go on one of those extreme family team-building ventures where everyone slides off a cliff, please be careful. And, stay hydrated!

Let's Do Some Good

This option is highly recommended. It will teach the whole family a lot about giving back to society, about appreciating each other and what you have, and it will inspire you to work even harder to become a tightly-knit group of individuals who love and respect one another.

Volunteer work is not something that is done by a lot of people, and organizations like homeless shelters and animal shelters always need volunteers. Even old-age homes will always appreciate an extra hand—not to mention all the elderly that live there who haven't seen their relatives for so long.

Making a difference in the lives of others can teach you a lot about yourself, especially your ODD child or teen. For example, they may realize that they have a lot of struggles in their life, but they also have a lot to be thankful for, like a family who supports them, a roof over their heads, and a yummy meal ready when they're home from school. It's truly heartwarming to show compassion to someone else. If your children like animals, take them to a shelter and let them play with and feed the animals. Some animals become really stressed if they are in a small enclosure for too long, so if you have older children or teens, you can organize for them to take the animals for walks or play with them outside their enclosures. For a child who hates authority and automatically rebels against it, how will it feel to work with those who have so much less than they do? It can have a huge impact on their frame of reference, and the whole experience can make you stronger as a family.

The Dinner Co-op

I could do with some pizza right now. Not the type that's delivered at your doorstep in 15 minutes—that pizza you make in your own kitchen where you start with the dough, chop up all the toppings, and watch it slowly cook in the oven with your mouth watering. Does your family like pizza? Have you ever made your own pizza at home? It's the best because you can put anything you like on your pizza. Involving the whole family in making dinner and creating it into a family tradition is a productive way of strengthening family bonds and, there are activities that require all skill levels from washing the vegetables to frying the bacon to kneeing the dough.

You don't have to make pizza, though. That was just the first thought that popped into my head, probably because I'm a bit peckish. If you have a specific cultural dish you enjoy as a family, then what a wonderful way to bring everyone together to work as a team. And the best part is enjoying the feast that all of you worked on afterward.

Beautiful Parent, Take Note

These activities are meant to be fun, empowering, and emotionally valuable to your family. However, you are constantly aware that you have a child or teen present that can blow up, defy instruction, and act negatively. For this reason, it is crucial to always be in control of the situation. If it's you and your partner, you can work as a team to keep the atmosphere the way you want it to. It's important to use positive reinforcement equally on all your children and not let it stand out that the whole operation is "Operation ODD." Your children may sense that and their reaction to your positive attempts may flip them around and worsen the situation. This is one of the most important things to keep in mind if you have an ODD child or teen. In the beginning, before you start implementing some of the behavioral techniques we discussed, you will still be walking on that thin line, not knowing when, why, or how the explosion will occur. What makes you a powerful parent is that you can rise above this, understand that it's something that can happen, but you can work toward making a massive improvement in your child's life.

Chapter 5:

Your ODD Child

There are behavioral aspects that overlap between a child with ODD and a teen with ODD, but there are also differences because they are in different phases of development. The age of an ODD child is usually between 5 and 12, which can make their level of understanding their actions when they are diagnosed still very limited. There is a big difference between a 6-year-old's understanding of ODD and a 15-year-old's understanding thereof. This is most likely due to the difference in brain development between a young child and a teenager combined with the hormonal phases a teenager's brain and body is experiencing that a young child is not. To understand the backdrop of ODD, let's look at how a child's brain develops, specifically when it comes to processing emotion in their younger years.

What's Happening Up There?

A child's ability to experience and express emotions develops at a rapid speed from as young as post-birth, and these abilities also include the child's capacity to manage and deal with different feelings. The most important part of a child's emotional development and social competence is said to occur between their birth up to the age of five, and the development that occurs in this period is linked to their ability to process emotions and develop meaningful relationships throughout their childhood and as adults. Parents and teachers tend to focus on a child's cognitive development and not so much on their emotional needs, which can influence their ability to deal with emotions throughout their lives. For many young children, understanding and processing simple emotions can be harder than learning to count or to read; however, the focus is seldomly shifted to this part of the child's neural development. Researchers at the Center of the Developing Child at Harvard University goes as far as to say that many opportunities for interventions that could have proved beneficial when dealing with future psychological issues in children are overlooked due to this faulty shift in focus.

The most elemental components of emotional development include a child's ability to identify and comprehend their own feelings, to be able to understand the emotions others are experiencing, to develop the ability to control strong emotions and express them in a way that is not destructive, to develop the ability to regulate their own behavior and develop empathy for those around them, and to develop the ability to establish meaningful and lasting relationships with others. These abilities are part of a child's neural infrastructure and its development is largely dependent on the environment the child is exposed to. Emotion is part of a child's biological development that is connected or wired into various parts of the central nervous system, which shows a long history of evolutionary development. Young children's emotional experiences during these development years become embedded in the wiring of their brains, almost like a tattoo. This is why the emotional development and healthy emotional development of young children can be life-changing for them; it is so closely tied to the emotional and social components of the environments they exist in. Environmental components that can influence a young child's emotional development include their parents, their extended families, the community they live in, and the experiences they have in these environments.

Although young children are still at a developmental stage emotionally, the depth of their emotions can be startling. They can experience intense feelings of anxiety, grief, sadness, depression, and anger, which can result in a manifestation of unmanageable anger or aggression. On the contrary, their highs can be just as intense and infectious, and for which children are normally better known.

It is important to also note that a child's temperament plays an important role in how they end up developing strategies to control their emotions at these early ages. However, temperament is not affected by one's environment; it is a biological component of a child's character and personality. For example, a child can be very shy and sensitive and be upset easily by something that wouldn't usually upset other children. On the contrary, the child may be more insensitive, prone to taking chances, and adventurous. Do any of these traits sound familiar to you? These temperaments pose different challenges to parents as they will have to customize their response to the child's temperament to ensure optimal development. If you have more than one child and they have different temperaments, it can become a tricky situation if you want each child to have the ideal support for their emotional development. When you look at it from a scientific perspective, it seems almost impossible to raise a healthy child, never mind children, and make a living altogether.

When looking at how a child's mind develops and processes emotion and how there are parts of a child's biological makeup that is going to influence this process that we as parents cannot change, there are a few things we can learn from looking at the development of the young child's mind.

First, research has established that there needs to be a focus on your child's emotional development when they are very young until they are at preschool age as these can be the make-or-break years which ingrains deep-set emotional experiences into the wiring of your child's brain that will affect the way they process and express emotions for the rest of their life. At the same time, your child is born with a temperament which will also influence the way they deal with and regulate emotions.

This being said, if young children's emotional development were more closely monitored, the need for intervention could have been identified in many cases where children eventually developed behavioral and psychological disorders. This increased focus and acts of intervention may not have completely eradicated these mental issues, but there is a possibility that the child's level of struggle would not have been so extreme. What do you think about this? Looking back at the time when your child was very young, do you think that there were possible warning signs in your child's behavior that could justify this scientific opinion? (National Scientific Council on the Developing Child, 2004)

Social Referencing

Social referencing is an interesting concept that influences a young child's development in many ways. A basic definition of social referencing would be the process a young child or an infant goes through to where they read the emotive displays or responses of their parents or caregivers in order to regulate their own way of responding to the world around them. This method of observation becomes a mechanism for the child to learn how to perceive, react, and feel about different components in their environment, and thereby create a framework for further exploration of the world out there. An example most parents will be familiar with is their young child's reaction when they fall or hurt themselves slightly. Their first reaction will be to observe the look on your face so they can determine how severe the situation is, and that would determine their own reaction to how they feel about hurting themselves. It can be quite comical. So, if your child trips and falls and you run to them with an upset face and a frantic voice, chances are they will start screaming and crying. However, if you smile and say "oopsie doopsie! let's get up and come to mommy" in a chirpy voice, they are more likely to disregard what just happened and continue with their day unperturbed. This is how your child uses your emotions and your emotional reactions to regulate their own emotional responses. And, don't be fooled, your baby starts checking you out from the age of 6 months!

From the ages of 6 months to 2 years, your child is extremely impressionable and dependent on your emotional state and emotional reactions to create their own frame of reference. For example, when your child is between the ages of 1 and 2, they will first wait for and then take your cues before approaching a new or foreign object. Similarly, they will first observe your facial expression and other emotional cues like your tone of voice before reacting to an unknown situation. Imagine the influence you have on your child's sense of perception and their ability to connect certain emotions with certain situations. This is a completely normal process and the information is not meant to be upsetting or accusative, but it is helpful for parents to be aware of it, especially if one or both parents suffer from anxiety or depression, for example. In cases like these, you may be sending your young child messages that you don't intend to because of a condition you have yourself, and this situation, that is no-one's fault, can affect your child's emotional development. There is the biggest mountain that ever existed that lies between a smile and a frown if it comes from their parents. The one makes them really happy and the other makes them really sad. When it comes to understanding social referencing and how it influences your child, here are three things you need to know:

- Social referencing is an essential component of your young child's emotional development. This is the time your child starts to understand the difference between emotional expressions, the sounds, words and tones that connect with them, and they use these references as their own to make associations with the world around them.

- Social referencing forms a fundamental part of your child's decision-making abilities, and your child's confidence and understanding of emotions are formed by your inputs.

- Social understanding lays a foundation for toddlers that allows the development of more complex thought, connotations, and the understanding of different emotional expressions. The influence at this age is much more profound than it is obvious on the child's development.

Make the Most of Social Referencing

Although social referencing is at its most influential for a child between 6 months and 2-3 years, it is still an ongoing process that you can use to help your child cope with difficult situations and problems they are experiencing in their own lives. It's another way of using positivity to influence and help your child, and now we know how deep this influence can go. In a way, it's a bit daunting to think that every gesture, facial expression, every time you speak or act, your child will, on a subconscious level, use it as a frame of reference–social reference. It's daunting because we know that we're not perfect and that one way or another, we're going to project an unhealthy reference when we are feeling irritated, tired, or overworked. Giving it a shot and being aware of controlling your actions, words, and facial expressions, you can still make a difference if your child is feeling anxious, depressed, sad, or angry. Consider these guidelines for clear social referencing in any environment with your youngster.

- When playing with your child or when you have the opportunity to interact face-to-face, use your facial expressions to teach your child emotive positivity. If your child is still very young, you can make several different facial expressions to teach them about the world around them. In the case of your older ODD child, use the opportunity to shine all of the love, affection, and acceptance you can muster through your eyes. Smile, and show your child that they needn't worry about you.

- When you're hanging out with your friends, remember that your little one is still watching you if they're around. They may be particularly curious as to how you conduct yourself in social situations. These situations are tricky because your child can become easily confused if your body language and tone of voice don't sync like they usually do when your little one is around. So, if you 'pretend' to like someone or act disingenuously, your child will immediately pick up on this emotion, and it will confuse the framework they've developed up to that point.

- The final point connects with the previous one; the way you react towards other people, situations, and different events has a very powerful effect on your child's perceptive development. For example, not losing your temper, staying positive in a frustrating situation, and being honest but polite are all qualities you'd want your child to learn, right? They are, however, not easy to demonstrate. Showing your child that you're trying and not giving up is also very valuable if you are in a situation where you just couldn't stay calm until the end–your child saw you actively trying. Additionally, when you are sad, show your child that expressing these emotions is not a bad thing; however, one needs to let it out and then let it go. You are your child's idol, so you can show them what is good, what is bad, what is healthy, and what is toxic through the way you act.

Just as you would use positive reinforcement and other types of behavioral conditioning systems to curb your child's aggression now that they are a bit older, also keep in mind the vast impact that social referencing had and still has on your child. You can choose to be mindful of the messages you send your ODD child, and if they are still very young, this can be a very helpful molding tool for their emotional development (Achwal, 2020).

How to Use this Information

Finally, we should keep in mind that oppositional defiant disorder's cause is not singular and the environmental factor is not the only identified influence. There is a neurological component that should also be considered; however, the neurological component cannot be influenced except with psychiatric medication. Emotional conditioning and support is something you as a parent can offer to help your child, and by understanding the depth of a young child's emotional processing and how it intertwines with their temperament, you may just be able to develop the best individual strategy yet for helping your ODD youngster. As the scientists say, when it comes to finding the best approach for raising your children, there is no "one size fits all" solution. And I think you'll agree with me, when it comes to raising a child with oppositional defiant disorder, this is a resounding reality (National Scientific Council on the Developing Child, 2004).

If you feel that there may have been times when your child was not in the ideal environment, whether it be socio-economically or among family members or friends, don't beat yourself up about it. There are remedies you can use now, and it's never too late to make a change. Don't blame yourself for situations that are or were out of your control, but always be proactive and on the lookout for the best opportunities for your child. Finally, if you decide to take your child to a professional for an assessment, make sure to provide them with any details you think may be relevant after reading this discussion about how children's emotional development can be affected. Any details about your child's earlier development that are possibly relevant to their emotional issues can help a professional make an accurate diagnosis.

Chapter 6:

Your ODD Teen

Understanding what's going on in your teenager's mind is important for understanding their ODD, especially at the different developmental stages of puberty. No definitive line has been drawn between teenage ODD and the hormonal development that takes place during puberty, but this information may end up being very useful in understanding your teenager overall and knowing when their behavior is full-on ODD and when it's just normal teenage rebellion. Let's take a look at a scientific perspective on puberty, emotional processing, and behavior.

What's Happening Up There?

As your child enters puberty, which can be from the age of 12 or 13 and can also depend on their gender, hormonal fluctuations will start to take place in areas of their brains that process and manage emotions and emotional responses. The first changes take place deep within the brain and then move to the most critical area that is located behind the forehead called the prefrontal cortex; this area in the brain is in control of your teen deciding whether they are going to lose their temper or throw a tantrum, among other reactions. The brain of a teenager or adolescent is completely unique as it cannot be described as a smaller version of an adult's brain or a bigger version of a child's brain. There are some unique things going on in there, which is why many adults tend to describe teenagers as a species on their own.

Most areas in the brain connected with emotional processing mature quickly from childhood; however, the prefrontal cortex takes a bit longer to process, leaving these other areas to their own devices. The prefrontal cortex in the adult brain is used for decision-making purposes, which can include how to react when being emotionally triggered. However, a teenager uses their amygdala when dealing with emotions because the prefrontal cortex has not reached the point where it is ready to take over the processing.

A hormone that starts to rise and affect both boys and girls during adolescence is testosterone. Tests conducted by neuroscientists indicated that testosterone is not only one of the driving forces that changes the teenage brain during puberty but that it is also closely associated with how capable an adolescent is of controlling their emotions effectively. Normally, testosterone is associated with males during puberty and the development of male physical characteristics. Now we know that, during puberty, testosterone is also responsible for reorganizing the brain, and it helps to control how the different structures in the brain develop in male and female brains during puberty.

Tests were conducted on male and female teenagers aged 14 where their ability to control their emotions was evaluated by conducting brain scans. Researchers found that teenagers with higher levels of testosterone in their brains had an increased capability to control their emotions due to their ability to access the prefrontal cortex. However, those with lower levels of testosterone appeared to rely heavily on the limbic system in this regard, which researchers say resembles the type of neural reaction one would see in a child's brain. In an ideal situation where the brain is fully developed, the prefrontal cortex would automatically regulate the limbic system in an emotionally-provoking situation. This study is a clear indication that teenagers have a natural tendency to struggle with controlling their emotions–some more than others.

And, if you combine hormones in the brain with other hormonal fluctuations, especially those that regulate adolescents' sexual development and sexual health, you know that there must be a lot going up there. A summary of the hormonal house party going on in your teenager's head includes the release of adrenal stress hormones, sex hormones, and growth hormones, which also contribute to the development of the teenage brain. Apart from looking at how testosterone and other hormones transform the adolescent brain, let's take a look at all the antics teenagers tend to get up to and their reasoning behind being the way they are, which can be so closely associated with ODD behavior.

Studies have indicated that the development of a teenager's intellectual abilities is very much the same as an adult's. However, their emotional development still lags behind and it is highly influenced by impulsivity, sexual drive, and thrill-seeking. In another discussion from a Harvard-published article, researchers again stress the importance of the prefrontal cortex, the limbic system, and the amygdala as components of the emotional processing system in the brain. The article also mentions that these parts of the brain reach their peak development stage when an individual reaches their early twenties. Thus, this is when a person would be able to, anatomically and developmentally, reach their full emotional-processing capacity. The brains of teenagers, on the other hand, are still undergoing this process, which can cause behavior that imitates that of clinically diagnosed ODD. Additionally, one of the reasons many addictions start during adolescence is because the part of a teenager's brain that regulates this 'reward' component is still under construction during this time, and many co-occurring conditions associated with ODD are also associated with the abuse of illicit drugs and alcohol (Harvard Health Blog, 2020; Brookshire, 2016).

So, why are we looking at this discussion that describes emotional processing and development in the teenage brain in so much detail?

First, if you have an ODD teen, then these hormonal inner workings may intensify their behavior and tantrums, so this is important to understand. If you know your teen well, you can try to discern between their normal teenage behavior and when it morphs into a serious ODD episode. This is valuable insight for a parent as it can determine how you should handle the situation. The majority of the discussion in this book lays the foundation for dealing with ODD children, although most of the information is also applicable to ODD teens. However, there is a need to treat teenagers differently when you discipline them because they are different than young children–their cognitive development is more advanced and they deserve to be treated as young adults, no matter their condition. This part of the book is specially dedicated to adding valuable information that can contribute to dealing more productively with your ODD teenager.

Discipline Differently

An ODD episode for a teen is about gaining control of a situation, and the situation can escalate rapidly if you are not experienced at handling such an episode. Teenagers don't necessarily want the same things from a relationship with their parents than a younger child. Because they are changing and they will soon be entering the adult world, they want to be respected, they want their opinion to be valued and respected, and they really want to be treated like an equal. Well, if your ODD child acts out in an immature way, this is hard to do, but there are ways to incorporate these approaches in the disciplining process.

An important approach you can incorporate into your method of discipline is to discipline a teenager with dignity. Just like it would be unprofessional to berate an employee in front of all their fellow employees, it's best to take the teen aside and discuss their bad behavior in private. This approach indicates that you are showing respect, and, whether they will show this or not, they will appreciate it. Disciplining an ODD teen in front of their peers will have a negative effect on their self-esteem, which is possibly already very low, and it opens up opportunities for bullying and ridicule. This, however, doesn't mean that you should be overly friendly or accommodating in your tone. The best way to get the message across is to approach the teen, discipline them by identifying the issue and the possible consequences, what you expect of them, and end it with a curt "thank you." This is all you need to do, and when you're done, you can break eye contact by turning around and walking away. It is very similar to the way you would handle an ODD child's misbehavior; you would not give them any type of negative reinforcement, but in the case of a teenager, they have the ability to understand their actions on a higher level, and because they expect you to treat them on this level, they should accept this treatment. If they try to provoke you after you've finished your part of the deal, you can nip it in the bud by simply ignoring it. It's tempting to turn around and give them a proper talking-to, but don't let them get to you, even if they try to get you in places that hurt.

Also, keep in mind that "keeping score" of everything an ODD teen does is going to cost you a lot of paper and it's not in any way productive or positive for their emotional development. For the teen, it may feel like they are sinking deeper and deeper into a hole that you are not allowing them to get out of, and this can be a source of negative reinforcement that may cause them to think, "Aw, what's the use? They're not going to let this go anyway." Consequently, they'll just keep on misbehaving, and their behavior can even get consistently worse along with their feeling of sinking deeper and deeper into their misbehavior hole, which makes them feel that they are losing control. Thus, even if your ODD teen tends to do the same infuriating things every day, start each day afresh for the sake of their mental health. No matter what terrible thing your teen did yesterday, you've dealt with it, most likely in the appropriate manner. Now, you can start the new day with an affectionate gesture and positive encouragement.

Teens are smart. ODD teens are not only smart, but they look for ways to use their smartness against you. If you want to curb this smart-alec behavior, there should be consequences for their smart actions. However because they are so smart, these consequences must be fool-proof and, most importantly, fail-proof. ODD children and naturally rebellious teens intensely dislike consequences and they do not react to them the same way other children do as I think parents with ODD children and teens very well know. An ODD teen will find ways to not only bend rules, but use your own words against you to turn a situation around. Sounds familiar? Here is an example of a "fail-proof" consequence: where you would just normally have confiscated a naughty teenager's phone, this won't do for your ODD teen. You're going to have to go the extra mile, and then another extra one. Pack some snacks. Because your child will search every corner of the property for that phone, eventually find it and refuse to give it back. You can be one step ahead by shutting off their phone service, which will make the phone completely useless to them. If they have to sit detention, sit outside the school and wait for your teen to sneak out the door so you can direct them straight in again. And again. Again, I advise you to buy some snacks for the occasion. You can work with your child's teacher to ensure your naughty teen attends the whole detention session (Balance, 2019).

This is not to be cruel but to be consistent. I think that by the end of the book, you'll know how to spell consistency, among other words, backward, which is one of my goals for you as an ODD parent.

How to Use this Information

Teenage ODD is in many cases very much like a younger child's ODD, but how it should be dealt with is a component that is different and, therefore, gets its own discussion. The above illustration of how to implement a fail-proof consequence shows one the level a teenager is on, and this takes communication and discipline to another level. A teenager requires a balanced approach when you are communicating with them; talking to them like they are children will infuriate them and might just as well serve as a trigger for misbehavior. So, even if punishment is being served, it needs to be served 'respectfully' in a way, as illustrated above. For example, even though you know you're going to say no to something, you still need to hear them out just for the sake of giving them that 'adult' treatment. It's hard to treat an ODD teenager like an adult in some ways because the way they tend to act is incredibly childish and defiant. However, this is where we need to realize that it's most likely not them but their disorder, and an active separation needs to be done in order to get the best behavioral results from your ODD teen. It is evident that there's a lot going on in a teenager's brain and a lot of changes are taking place. They are also starting to use their brains differently than children, and even though they don't have a complete grasp on using their emotional processing system in the brain yet, they're moving in that direction. Other issues like impulsivity affect them more. Let's take this into consideration.

Chapter 7:

Am I Missing Something?

One component within a family that is often neglected to the despair of all members is the parental unit. Whether there is only one parent or whether there are two, their health and well-being should also be a priority in order for them to raise a child with a behavioral disorder. This is where parents often misinterpret how to organize their priorities solely for not wanting to neglect their children or cause them any harm. You know, you just love your children too much, so how does it make sense to focus on yourself and to focus on your relationship with your partner if one of them needs help? Within a family context, no matter what the circumstances, there should be a time and a place for everything, and each member has the right to practice self-care and to do things that enrich them physically and spiritually to maintain a high level of health. Once parents understand the importance of self-care for themselves, they can fully understand how their health influences the health of their children. Keeping up with the antics of an ODD child or teen is a challenging venture in itself. However, every night when you plop your head down on your pillow, you need to be able to say that you are actively working on your own health as well, for the sake of your child. Which scenario is better, the sick helping the sick or the healthy and strong helping the sick? By 'sick,' I mean that those who are overburdened with responsibility experience undue stress; you may not realize it and you may tell yourself that you're fine, but you need to do some maintenance. For your children's sake and for your partner's sake. Additionally, you and your partner can also set time aside to actively work on your relationship. If parents have a healthy relationship that they actively work on, their children are less likely to experience unnecessary stress due to fighting or tension. Why don't we use this chapter to focus on the parent, the cornerstone and architect of the family, and how parents can focus on their health and relationships with a little less guilt.

Look After Yourself!

Parents tend to underestimate self-care so often because they put the well-being of their children before their own. Naturally. However, there really is time you can take for yourself and not feel guilty, I promise you that. I know this because we as parents are all sometimes too concerned about our children and too dismissive about the benefits of practicing self-care. And, having a child that has specific issues makes it even more irrational and unjustifiable in your mind to take some time for yourself and spoil yourself. However, if this is the case, you may be looking at the big picture from upside down. We touched on this earlier when we discussed the 3 P's. Your focus on your own mental health as a parent is crucial if you have a child struggling with theirs. And, as a parent, we tend to think self-care is a selfish act because we could've used this time to somehow improve the lives of our children. It's a guilt trip's ultimate fantasy. If only parents knew that, if they took that time and focused on themselves, reinvigorate their minds and souls, and practice something they enjoy, then that will be exactly what they'll be doing! Because each of us is different, we are going to go through some very basic examples of self-care with the aim to spark some ideas in your minds of what you would like to do as an individual. I personally love some of these activities, and some I don't really enjoy, and it will probably be the same for you. So, take what you find enticing and make it your own while keeping the goal in your mind's eye—the well-being and happiness of your children.

Basic activity number one is taking time for yourself to reflect and meditate. If you find this activity attractive, there are some important things you need to consider to make the venture successful and rewarding. For meditation to work for you, you'll need to find a spot that is quiet, where you enjoy being in, and where you won't be interrupted or bothered by noise. The atmosphere will influence the quality of your sessions. You can sit up or lie down, just make sure that your body is comfortable enough for you to focus on your mind. Another idea for meditation is for you to create themes or topics you can focus on during each session. These can be related to family matters, to self-improvement, or they can even be completely transcendental of nature. Another idea is to use the time to train yourself in the art of mindfulness. Focus on relaxing and learning and love and embrace who you are.

The next activity has some interesting research linked to it. It involves taking alone time and spending it in a natural environment, like in a park, next to a lake, or in a forest. The interesting part involves research conducted on hospital patients, which found that patients who had windows next to their beds with a view of a garden or greenery healed faster than other patients. Nature just has that healing power. Also, how about combining your meditation session with spending time in nature? It might take more effort, but on the other hand, it can be very rewarding considering its mental healing properties. This is similar to the family hike activity idea, except this time you're going solo. Depending on where you live, you can take a stroll in the garden, next to the ocean on the beach, in the park, or you can fill a room in your house with greenery and just go and relax on the couch. It's your call.

Next up on our list of self-care ideas is creating a journal that is meant for entries containing positive thoughts and thoughts of gratitude only. You can always have a vent journal on the side, but let's focus on the positive one for now. And, keep it secret. Make time for yourself to be alone. Go and sit in a café and have your favorite drink. Let thoughts and ideas mull around in your head and then spill them onto your page. Don't think too much. Just let the positivity flow and think about all the things you've been able to accomplish, all your abilities, all your gifts and talents, and your beautiful children. Who you want to say thank you to is up to you. But experiencing that feeling of gratitude is healing and rebuilds the spirit and strength you nourish your family with. What is the first thing you would write in your journal?

There are so many simple ways you can help yourself to wind down and build up sustainable and multipurpose energy for those multipurpose moments that only a family with an ODD family member knows of. Here's another one; take some time to yourself and listen to music. Music has magical properties that we as mere men do not understand; it can enchant us, enrage us, give us energy, revive us, and put us to sleep. The choice of the music is up to you. You can rock 'n roll in your underwear in front of the mirror while your partner takes all the little ones out for ice cream, bellowing out Queen's "We Are the

Champions." Just remember to return the favor. Alternatively, you can find a place where you can lie down comfortably and listen to classical music through a device that has good sound quality. When I refer to classical music, I refer to composers whose music will transform you into another world of calm beauty. I, for example, love to listen to the French impressionist composer Claude Debussy. You can also opt for some light classical music or chanting. It depends on what puts you into a mode where nothing is scratching the inside of your mind. Fall asleep to it and take a nap–you'll soon be woken up by one of your children shoving an ice cream in your face.

The next option is one that everybody will love. But, nobody ever wants to do it because they don't feel that they deserve it. Introducing "spend a little something on yourself" as one of the ultimate self-care. However, let's give it a chance and inspect how we can make spending a bit of money on ourselves a reality. First, you need to identify what you'd want to spend the money on. I think we can all agree that we're going to have to be realistic here. So, if you enjoy grooming and pampering, then going for a facial treatment or a nail session may just be a great option for you. "But, where am I going to get the money?" she asks. That's a good question. If you don't currently have a lot of money, think about instances during the past few weeks when you bought yourself small but non-essential things, like candy. How many times did this happen? And, if you dare estimate how much all those purchases were together, do they come close to covering a new facial or nail session once or twice a month? Buying yourself candy can also be identified as spending money on yourself, but it just doesn't have that same effect. Especially since it doesn't relax and invigorate you– you may even feel some guilt hanging over your head when you see you've finished the whole pack. This self-care option is definitely possible, but it may require some budgeting. What you can give back to your family when you trade in those candy bars and sodas will make it worth it.

Finally, an invigorating option that comes to you last is to consider a short digital detox once or twice a week. Digital detoxing means that you cut out technology from your life for a certain period of time. You can decide when and for how long. Digital detoxing can also be good for healthy family bonding; for example, if no one is allowed their phones, iPads or other gaming devices at the dinner table, the family can focus on having real bonding time. However, as a self-care practice, this activity should be focused on you and how you can allow yourself to relax and spend quality time gaining back the strength one loses along the way when dealing with children's issues. So, how would you incorporate a digital detox as part of self-care? The great thing about all of these options is that they can be combined and used in conjunction with each other so everyone can find their perfect self-care activity or routine (Morin, 2020a).

Work on Your Partnership

After an extensive study conducted by married couple and co-academics Philip Cowan, Ph.D. and his wife Carolyn Pape Cowen, Ph.D., who were both professors in Psychology at the University of California in Berkeley, some interesting details have become more prominent about what happens to the relationship of a couple after they have children. Interestingly enough, the Cowens decided to initiate this study due to them identifying a decline in their relationship after having children of their own. This was in the 1970s. In 1975, the couple started the Deciding to Become a Family project, and they started tracking couples' relationships from before the birth of their first child until the child was ready to go to kindergarten. Then, in 1990, they started another project called the Schoolchildren and their Families Project, looking at the relationship between parents who have younger schoolchildren. The Cowens only completed their research and projects in the year 2005, but they have some insightful information to offer for couples who are planning to have children, couples with children, and couples with ODD children, like us. In most cases, a couple's relationship and marital satisfaction declines after having children, and according to their observations, this appears to have a negative influence on the child or children, especially emotionally and academically or when it comes to learning. However, there are couples who manage to maintain a sense of marital bliss even after they've had children, and the maintenance of this spark appears to be important for a child's well-being from a young age until they become young adults. If you have a child that is experiencing additional struggles and simultaneously causing havoc in your household, maintaining a solid foundation in your relationship as parents is clearly vital. So, if it doesn't always happen naturally and there are circumstances, like in the case where your child has a disorder, that can even further complicate things, what can parents do from their side to protect and nurture their relationship?

According to our experts, most of the couples from their first study reported that their marriage is in distress before their baby's second birthday, if they haven't filed for divorce already. These couples described their relationship after having a baby as one that experienced gradually increasing conflict until it came to that point of distress. So, if this seems to be a common issue, it's one we need to look at, study, and see if there is a solution if we want the best for our children. The Cowens subsequently spoke about marriages that did not experience any such issues after having children, and their feedback came down to a very simple concept. Couples who don't experience increasing issues after having children generally have the ability to manage communication and decision-making very well. A child as a new addition in a family brings along with it the contestation of new opinions, power struggles, possible trust issues, and if a couple can maintain a basic foundation of mutual respect, this can be a make-or-break factor in the relationship.

In this discussion, the Cowens are talking about parents with children who do not specifically have any chronic illnesses, disorders, or other complicating factors. However, the parents they refer to still seem to struggle to manage their own relationships even if their children are healthy. What the Cowens are saying to parents with ODD children, in other words, is that the level of trust and respect between partners and parents needs to be rock-solid, and they have to have each other's backs at all times. Just like how you'd want your ODD child to learn about teamwork in sports and in the family setup, parents need to work as a team to understand how important the health of their relationship is and how it can affect their children.

To put years of research into a nutshell, here is what these highly regarded academic individuals would advise you to do and not to do to form a strong partnership that can be the basis for raising a healthy child. Something that the Cowens noted that I found to be profoundly significant is that couples spend a lot of time and energy preparing for how they are going to deal with the birth of the baby. This, being a big and life-changing event, is completely understandable. However, they added that couples don't seem to give their post-birth as much thought, which is where conflict and disagreement arises. The birth of a child is not the only life-changing component of having children, but the entire process of raising them will have that same life-changing effect. Of course, when your child is born, you are not aware of the fact that they may develop a behavioral disorder, but being prepared as parents for the easy and hard times must surely be crucial for successful parenting and maintaining a loving relationship whilst doing so.

It is also important to understand how the way each parent was raised and their family contexts are going to affect their parenting styles, whether consciously or subconsciously, and it is crucial for parents to go easy on each other regarding this, except if the behavior is socially or ethically unacceptable. Overcompensation or projection are common parental behaviors that often happen on a subconscious level; however, if your partner in crime's primary reaction is going to be to judge you in these kinds of situations, the bond between you will suffer. Remember that both of you have your faults and your strengths, and being open and honest will bring the best out of your relationship and parenthood.

An interesting piece of advice offered by the Cowens that most of us have probably heard from other sources as well is for a couple to work on or deal with their issues or differences when they are both calm and not overly emotional. What makes this advice unique in this case is that it is based on decades of research by two experts in psychology. If you dismissed this idea in the past, maybe it's time to reconsider. I tend to think the reason we dismiss this idea so easily and leave it on the back-burner in our minds is because it is so incredibly difficult to master. To grab a hold of yourself and say, "I know you want to get all of this pent-up frustration out in the most immediate and satisfying way possible, but your own satisfaction is not what's important right now" is not what you want to hear when you are livid or frustrated to the point of no return, but what an accomplishment it will be for your family's health if you can leave it to cool down. You will, of course, require the cooperation of your partner, which is why there are marital mishaps so often. If it ever happens that you have an argument in front of your children, it is very important for them to know that you sorted out the issue if this didn't also happen in their presence. Children are extremely sensitive to the relationship dynamics between their parents, and if you have an ODD child or teen, keeping your arguments hidden from them is for their own good. If there is the slightest discord between you and your partner, your children can pick up on this, and it can have a negative effect on their development and happiness.

This is why a stable parental relationship is so extremely important if you have a child whose struggles can be overwhelming for them on their own. On a lighter note, this part of the discussion won't be complete without some tips on how to create an environment where you can cultivate a strong and healthy partnership.

Need Some Space?

You get clingy partners and you get semi-disconnected partners. If the one marries the other, how do you balance the space issue? The same goes for two clingy, jealous types in a relationship. There always needs to be a compromise. The clingy type may likely interpret the "I need some space" or "I'm just going for a quick drive on my own" as a "leave me alone." Especially if their partner says the words, "On my own!" On the other hand, their partner, who just wants to take the scenic route around town to clear his head about something that happened at work, may find it irrational if their partner can't seem to understand this. Space is important. You are one, but you are also two. It sounds simple, but when you think about it, it requires some digestion, and it will eventually need to be redigested as you encounter the same emotions about the same issue. If partners can reach the point where they understand that space is essential for maintaining a healthy relationship, they've reached a point of maturity in their relationship that will bring them happiness and prosperity. It's the same as being OK with your partner taking time to practice self-care. The trick here is to understand how much space your partner needs, to respect this, and to know that they need this space because they love you. In some cases, it will take some self-sacrifice for an extroverted partner to understand that their introverted partner needs a lot more alone time. But isn't that so much better than spending time together with your partner visibly irked or uncomfortable because they actually need alone time? Not giving each other space or developing feelings of resentment towards each other because of these needs can cause serious relationship damage, and besides, allowing your partner that time is the ultimate sign of love and respect.

Practice Couple Care

We've been around the self-care block. So, what's couple care all about? That's standing in for your partner when they need you. When you can see that they are on their wits' end with your child talking back again, and you just swoop in to do the rest of negotiation before they explode. Rubbing their shoulders when they've had a tough session at the gym. Pouring them a hot bath after a long day. Enjoying some good wine together. Or bourbon, gin, or tequila! Giving each other a good-night kiss. Giving each other a good-morning kiss. Taking turns in doing the laundry or the grocery shopping, or even doing it together.

Thinking twice before making a snide or insensitive remark. Telling them they look good and that they smell nice. Helping them when they need help. Having sex as often as your schedules permit you to. Discussing your children and co-parenting strategies. Holding hands. Cuddling. Smiling and laughing. Making a conscious effort to appreciate the small things. Communicating regularly. Being honest. And finally, valuing integrity in the relationship.

Sync Those Nervous Systems

Moving to a more primitive part of our human composition, syncing your nervous system with your partner's can provide a primal sense of connection. Never underestimate components that contribute to human relationships that may be considered primitive like hormones, neural pathways, body language, or, in this case, our nervous systems. This is one of those pieces of advice that may seem completely absurd because one won't necessarily experience an immediate or obvious effect from it. Let's describe it first before I create a false impression about an activity that is effective and influential. In order to achieve this nervous system sync, you need to hug your partner. First, make sure that you stand belly-to-belly, no talking, and relax into the hug until you can feel that both of your bodies are relaxed. By doing this simple act, your nervous system recalculates itself from feeling separated, disconnected and possibly vulnerable to reconnecting, making you feel safe again. That being said, while you are hugging your partner in this way, your nervous system is also calculating whether there are any changes from their side; for example, are they still connected, are they in a good or bad mood? More importantly, are you safe with your partner? It's like running an emotional MRI scan on your partner and on both of you to see if any issues can be detected and to primarily reconnect on a primal level. Syncing every morning before work or whenever you get a chance to give each other some affection, try this technique.

Agree on Default Check-ins

Tricky, tricky! We just discussed space, so what do you think about previously agreed-on check-ins? It can be optional, but it's part of the discussion because many couples benefit from having standard times that they check in with each other, especially if one partner is looking after the children, a partner has a long or dangerous commute home after work, or if anything unexpected comes up during the day that can be communicated during these check-ins. Some couples thrive on these types of systems and orderly ways of running their days, and others need more freedom to send impromptu messages. These types of check-ins also prove to be invaluable if parents are separated and times, dates, and locations need to be organized in terms of picking up the kids, communicating with each other when it comes to the kids' progress, behavior, health, and other relevant topics. Having default check-ins should, I daresay, be strongly considered if you and your partner are separated and you have children, and even more so if one of your children has ODD. Deciding to communicate at default times, to some extent, makes up for your choice to separate and shows that you are committed to co-parenting from your separated positions (Kruger, 2005; Morin, 2020).

In the end, it is imperative for parents with ODD children to understand how the health of their relationship plays a role in your child's response to treatment, whichever you choose for them. Teenagers, just as younger children, still need that sense of security from their parents or guardians, and they are extremely sensitive to any relationship discord between their parents. If you are a single parent or co-parenting but are divorced, it is even more important to establish a sense of security for your child, so their main focus can be getting better. A family is a complex unit that contains elements of individuality and unity; knowing when to focus on which aspect is a skill most parents acquire through trial and error. If there are more important issues to focus on, though, it's good to have some guidelines available that you can personalize and optimize in your familial context.

Keys to Understanding the ODD Diagnosis as a Parent

Understanding that your child is ill is difficult. However, understanding that your child has a behavioral disorder like ODD can really blow your mind because the manifestation of the illness is in an aggressive display of disdain, disrespect, and sometimes even what appears to be hatred. It is incredibly hard to fathom that this is your child's illness you are witnessing and not your child. Yet, knowing that your child is not the disorder and the disorder is not your child will make it easier for you to protect yourself against its negativity and provide your child with what they truly need: support, structure, and discipline without the drama. As a parent with an ODD child or teen, it is extremely important to understand the most basic concept that is affecting you right now: your child's ODD is more than bad behavior, and your ODD child doesn't have the ability to cooperate when they are acting out by throwing a tantrum or being aggressive. Secondly, it is imperative for a child who displays ODD symptoms to get a professional diagnosis and treatment. As we discovered at the end of the first chapter, untreated ODD can be detrimental to your child's health. So, the keys bring you to a point of understanding as a parent is to separate yourself emotionally from the situation, as hard as that may be, to understand that your child is not deliberately trying to hurt you, and to comprehend the idea that the aggressive behavior is linked to the disorder and not who your child really is. These three components will bring you the clarity you need to assist your child during difficult moments.

Find Support Groups – You're Not Alone

Apart from all the diverse details discussed in this book, you still may have questions about aspects of your child's life you would want to explore more, or you may even want to connect with other parents who also have children or teens with ODD. This is because every situation is unique, and there may be a very specific piece of information you are looking for, or you want to discuss a situation that you have not experienced or read about before and get feedback from other parents who are going through the same situation. Apart from possible support groups in your area, there are some valuable sources on the web you can keep bookmarked and discussion or support groups you can join online and on social media. Here are some of the best sites and groups you can consider joining or keeping closeby on your browser for day-to-day support and information:

- Two websites where you can find reliable and regularly-updated medical information about ODD that will always be current and relevant are, first, the *American Academy of Child and Adult Psychiatry* and *Cincinnati Hospital Center.* These sites are specifically handy when it comes to managing a child who has both ODD and co-existing conditions like ADHD or anxiety. These sites can also help you to distinguish between ODD and a co-occurring condition that may require the same management techniques but it's still important to distinguish between the two conditions and their diagnoses.
- If you want to look for ideas regarding any aspect of ODD, living with an ODD child, ODD management, and more, there are three great sites that will most likely meet your needs. The first site is *Lives in the Balance,* which aims to provide collaborative and proactive solutions for children with

behavioral disorders and other issues. Second, the site *DocSpeak* is a go-to if you have any questions regarding living and co-existing with an ODD child or teen. Then, a site that you may find very useful, especially during those moments when you feel you've hit a brick wall, is *Transforming the Difficult Child* or difficultchild.com. Here, you can find a treasure chest full of ideas and different approaches that can possibly fit your situation and circumstances in a more specific way that would otherwise have been described in an ODD guide.

- This site is especially helpful if you have an ODD teen and you are struggling to manage their normal, more hormonal teenage behavior along with the symptoms of ODD. If you need extra advice, some supportive words, or you just need to read about teenage-related ODD specifically, then this is your go-to (Mauro, 2020).

- Reading about ODD is not always going to be enough. Talking to parents who are going through the same situation you are going through can be incredibly therapeutic and fulfilling. If you don't have this opportunity in the area where you live, there are some brilliant ODD support groups on social media like Facebook. Some are open groups and some are closed. Most of these support groups have more than 5K members and there are also support groups for parents with ODD children who have co-occurring disorders like ADHD or anxiety disorder. There are support groups for single parents specifically, and there are support groups that link ODD with other challenges like homeschooling. Groups that are worth looking at on Facebook include *Support for parents of children with ODD (Oppositional Defiance Disorder)*, which is a private group with about 25k members. They have been around since 2012, and they have well-established and solid group rules that involve conduct and communication. Another group similar to the first one but with fewer members is *PARENTS Of OPPOSITIONAL DEFIANT DISORDER CHILDREN.* This is also a closed group, which has been around for quite a few years (2013), with well-established group rules and about 14k members. It may be possible that you'd want to join a group with fewer members as so many members in a group can flood the chat section. If you want to look at less crowded options, there's *Oppositional defiant disorder (ODD) parent support group*. This group has just over 5k members; however, you have to answer a set of questions before you'll be allowed to join. This group is quite younger as it was established in 2017, but also appears to be organized.

A great option for single parents is the *Oppositional Defiant Disorder (ODD) Single Parent Support Group* which is created specifically for single parents to communicate about their unique struggles. This private group has been around since 2014 and has some reasonable ground rules. If you're looking for an ODD and ADHD combined group, you can look at *ADD & ODD Parent Support (Oppositional Defiant Disorder). All of these groups are on Facebook, and you can search them by using the words ODD/Oppositional defiant disorder support groups.*

- There's another source you can use that's quite unique in the way that you get your information through a content creator, but a lot of subscribers like to request specific topics, so if there's something you would like to know, there's also an avenue for you to get this information using this medium. Many of these content creators are also professionals and experts in their field, so the information you get through this medium may be of a different value than getting emotional support from parents who are in the same situation as you are. This is, of course, listening to podcasts and looking for channels on platforms like YouTube that discusses ODD, ODD parenting, and all the related aspects of dealing with it and managing the difficult situations. If you are interested in looking into following a respectable channel, I have lined up a few for you that you can take a look at to see if any of them fits your specific needs.

The first channel that is worth taking a look at is *ADDitude Magazine*'s YouTube channel. It focuses mainly on ADHD, but there are a lot of videos that discuss ODD and can provide valuable information from a professional's perspective. Another channel that is from a family's perspective is *BonnieandTom Liotta*. This channel discusses a range of issues from a family's perspective that seems to have successfully dealt with ODD in their own environment. Finally, you can also take a look at *tvoparents* as a channel that has multiple episodes discussing ODD from different perspectives. There are other channels out there, so you don't even have to choose a channel; you can just watch videos that appear interesting or informative to you.

Chapter 8:

How to Discipline my ODD Child

or Teenager

We've all been through this. We've tried multiple strategies with the aim to discipline our ODD child or teen without becoming emotional, angry, overly upset, or just plain losing it. If you've done a lot of research and tried many approaches, chances are that you may have tried one that would've eventually worked, but the hard part is to stick to it when your child or teen is being so incredibly difficult. And, the most infuriating and unfathomable part of dealing with an ODD child or teen is that, even though you, as the parent, need to remind yourself that it is a condition and that your child's destructive and abrasive behaviors are not who they really are, they still seem to know exactly how and when to push your buttons and will never hesitate to do so when they lash out. This is what leaves ODD parents so tired, defeated, and sometimes even completely depressed; wrapping your head around that paradox is not easy, and parents that deal with this on a daily basis should be commended for actively trying to understand their child's situation while being under constant attack. There are two key components to effectively disciplining an ODD child or teen. The first is using techniques that have proven to be effective and that are not emotionally harmful to your child. Secondly, and this is where most parents falter just because it is so incredibly hard: consistency. Don't leave even a crack open where your child can identify a gap and take their chances to act out. Start by considering these fundamental strategies you can implement in your household to tame your child's aggression and anger by drastically limiting their opportunities to misbehave.

Fundamental Strategies

Let's state the facts. Children and teenagers with ODD are blatantly and unabashedly disrespectful, confrontational, and disobedient. So, how do you curb this destructive behavior that is affecting everyone in your household? Understanding their behavior and reacting based on that understanding is key.

Positive Attention

First, one of the things that can make ODD behavior worse is if the child sees that they are negatively reprimanded more than their siblings. This essentially means that their brain will wire itself to think their siblings always get positive attention and they always get negative attention, which can cause feelings of bitterness or jealousy. And, these feelings are going to worsen their behavior. So, when you see your child or teen acting up, try to stop what you are doing to give them your attention for at least fifteen minutes. Try to smother the aggression and defiance with positivity and affection, and depending on their age, do a quick activity with them or ask them to do something that will make them feel special. This approach is almost the same as one we've previously discussed where the negative behavior of the child is completely ignored. However in this case, you will use this approach if you know that the behavior exhibited may be due to neurological interplay, for example, ADHD acting up or if you could see that your child was clearly triggered.

The Behavior Plan/Reward System

The second strategy can be successfully linked to the first one to create a multifaceted prevention approach. The second strategy is to create an action and consequence behavior plan that you can discuss with your child. This will work well if your child is old enough to understand the concept, but considering the general age range of children diagnosed with ODD, it is unlikely that your child will be too young.

Start creating the plan by identifying the behavioral issues that need to be addressed. These issues can range from acting aggressively towards you, your partner, or siblings, refusing to follow any orders or doing schoolwork, shouting or saying nasty things, throwing tantrums, or misbehaving at school. After you've identified the pressing behaviors, you need to identify fitting consequences that are aimed at improving your child's understanding of their behavior but also not breaking down their self-esteem. There could be rewards if they behave and maybe some extra chores if they don't. A reward system is something that has been tried out in a disciplinary strategy for ODD children, and it has proven to be successful over and over again. There are different types of reward systems parents use, and many parents come up with their own unique ideas and systems that fit their household requirements. However, there are also systems that already have established procedures and rules, like the token economy system that works well with ODD children and teens, so let's take a look at this reward system as an example.

How to Create a Token Economy System in Your Household

A token economy system is known as one of the most effective ways to get any child to follow your house rules, and this includes children with ODD. However, there may still be a slight delay in compliance if your child has ODD, but the success has been proven. This system works like an action and consequence behavior plan, but it has a built-in rewards system. Your children earn tokens for reaching specific goals on a daily, bi-daily, or weekly basis, and the tokens work almost like a monetary system that they can use to claim or buy bigger rewards. If your child is still in kindergarten, you can consider using a sticker chart as they really enjoy this format, but if your child is older, the tokens work very well. Let's say, for example, you want your child to complete their homework in the afternoon, come home from school with no complaints from their teachers, go a week without any temper tantrums, or do their chores. They can earn tokens for doing what is expected of them, and these tokens then have a specific value. Linked to earning the tokens, you can have a system indicating what they can "earn" or which rewards they can get with x number of tokens. These rewards can start small for a small number of tokens, and can become more valuable and covetable for a larger number of tokens. By choosing rewards that you know your children love, they'll be motivated to behave, get the tokens, and save up for their rewards. So, if we want to create a token economy, where do we start?

- Keep it simple. Parents can get really hyped up about creating a rewards system or a token economy system, and this can result in lots of planning and an elaborate setup, which ends up looking almost like a business pitch! The problem is, it is going to completely confuse your child. Approach the creation of the system by looking at it from your child's perspective; you know your child better than anyone, so as long as you keep in mind that the system is being created for your child and why it's being created, your efforts will most likely be wildly successful.

- Now, you need to determine the goals your child needs to achieve in order to earn tokens. Pour yourself a glass of wine and mull over this for a while. You don't want your child to think that some good behavior is more valuable or 'better' than others; you'd rather want to create the impression that all good behavior is equal. If you want to give your child tokens of different values for different goals without creating this impression, you can place the focal point on effort. Alternatively, all tokens can have the same value, and your child will just have to save longer for larger rewards; it doesn't have to be that complicated.

- Next, a component that is important to consider is to not only focus on bad behavior and giving your ODD child goals that are tough to achieve. They are going to struggle with most of their behavioral goals, and they will need motivation by earning tokens for other behavior or activities that they do not find as difficult to complete or achieve. So, when you draw up your goals that will get your ODD child their tokens, make sure that there is one easily attainable goal and some intermediate goals hidden in between. Depending on your child's age, it's also a good idea to consider how many behaviors you want to include in your system at one time based on whether your child will find a system with several behaviors or activities confusing or not.

- This point is just a reminder to remember the number one most important requirement when dealing with an ODD child, which is positivity. As with every other aspect, this system needs to be approached in a positive way, and the "difficult" goals should not be framed as reprehensible or repugnant behavior. Your child's behavior indicates in itself the amount of negativity they experience within themselves, so the more you can envelop them with positivity, the better. Help them to interpret these behaviors as aspects that can be improved, but not as traits they have because they are bad individuals. Every goal in the token economy system is equal in its value; however, you may consider implementing your own interpretation of the rewards regarding how much effort the child needs to put in to achieve it. Also note that, if you want to use the effort component to create tokens of different values, the concept of effort needs to be logically quantifiable. An incorrect way of interpreting the effort here would be to say that Annie worked "twice as hard," so she gets a token with a higher value. Avoid any abstract ideas when it comes to calculating and estimating rewards and tokens as children have a hard time understanding these abstract concepts.

- When a child earns a token, be present to hand it over in a congratulatory fashion. If you're going to handle this part of the process by telling your child, "Go get your token; it's on top of the fridge," there's an important element missing; the element where you physically acknowledge your child's achievement, which is vital to the systematic improvement of their behavior.

- Some other useful ideas are to help your child identify a special designated token container. This will work especially well with younger children as it will make the whole idea even more official and legitimate. You can go all out and decorate a jar or a container, stick on a label, and place it in a spot in the house where everyone can see it or in your child's room if they prefer it to be there.

- Choose a type of token that your child cannot find anywhere in the home and secretly add their own in the token jar. If you were to use marbles as tokens, your child may likely be able to source some marbles from a friend and secretly add them to the token jar. Now, we're not saying they'll do this, but you know kids. A good example of tokens you can use are poker chips. You can also make your own tokens; just make sure that your child doesn't have access to them.

- If you want your token economy system to veer away from a materialistic venture, you can focus on coming up with rewards that don't cost money or that are not based on monetary status. For example, giving your child the newest PlayStation as a reward is likely going to create the impression that they'll expect something even bigger next time. Keep this in mind when you think about which rewards you want to give your children. The rewards can also teach them a lot about life and that not everything is about money. However, you still want them to enjoy the rewards, otherwise the whole token economy idea may collapse.

- Although a token economy system is generally very successful when used with ODD children and teens, you may encounter a few bumps in the beginning. You can prepare yourself for the most common token economy system issues beforehand so you'll be ready to fix them if they should occur. One of the issues that you may have been thinking about while reading this discussion is that your child may not be interested in earning any tokens because they don't like the rewards that are being offered. If this is the case, you can consider discussing the rewards with your child and reaching a compromise that doesn't cross any of your boundaries, which could be a specific amount of money you're prepared to spend or something you are prepared to do. It may also be hard for your child to get the feel of the token economy system if they have a lot of privileges and are used to getting the things they ask for. Try using these privileges, for example allowing them to play video games, as rewards.

- If you have more than one child, don't exclude the others from the token reward economy system. You can create some healthy competition and relationship-building by advertising the system as a positive way for your kids to work together and to give each child an easy, intermediate, and difficult goal to achieve. There can even be challenges where your kids need to work together in order to get their tokens, and you can call it a "group challenge."

- Finally, depending on what is available to you and what you've already made available to your child, try to provide a variety of rewards throughout the weeks as children can get bored easily. You can help them manage their "reward wealth" by using the tokens now for smaller rewards or by giving them bigger rewards that they will have to save up for, which means long-term good behavior

Establish Clear-Cut Rules

Rules are probably the things your ODD child loves complaining and arguing about the most because they become a convenient platform for an argument or a tantrum. They are usually also very vigilant when it comes to parents setting out the rules–if there's a loophole somewhere, they'll find it, and you will know the second they think something is unfair. So, this is a component that is separate from any rewards system you decide to implement in your house; this is about setting the ground rules. To avoid any "you said, they said" situations, create a rule card or document that clearly sets out all the rules, and stick it against the fridge or the back door where the whole family can see it.

If you want the rule list to be effective, don't make it too long, always refer to it with respect and refer to a family member who broke the rules with respect, and include basic rules that include chores, schoolwork, and family communication. Finally, make sure not to break any of the rules yourself and then be dismissive about it–this would ultimately destroy any attempt at getting your ODD child to understand why they have to follow the rules.

Don't Fall for Power Struggle Provocation

If you have an ODD child or teen, you know that your authority is being tested regularly. Children and teenagers with ODD love to and are good at trapping authority figures in ongoing arguments or debates about what they may find to be unfair or troublesome. However, if you have a household with a solid rule system that applies to everyone, there is no need to entertain your ODD child or teen in such an extended argument about their interpretation of right and wrong. If you've discussed the house rules with the family, including all of your children, and the necessary questions were answered, then there's no need to respond to unproductive power struggles.

Here is an example of what you can do. If you give your ODD child or teen a clear instruction to, for example, wash the dishes, and they try to argue back, move on straight to the consequence set for that action if you are confident that your instruction was clear. Your child will start an argument with you about washing the dishes because that's going to delay them actually having to go to the kitchen and wash the dishes. Don't fall for this delay tactic; make sure that your child understands the instruction, and if they don't comply, remind them of the consequences before enforcing it.

The point here is not to force your child into doing things they don't want to do, but it is more about maintaining fair and reasonable household rules. Giving them negative attention is going to feed their reactive tendencies, so just ensure that they are reminded of the house rules and that it is enforced if they do not do their part. When it comes to effectively dealing with ODD, you have two best friends that will always have your back: positivity and consistency (Morin, 2020b).

Consistency, Consistency, Consistency

It can't be said enough. ODD children thrive on loopholes, inconsistent behavior from authority figures and even their peers, and taking a gap when they see one. Your system should be as watertight as Noah's ark; however, instead of its requirements being to hold out water for forty days and forty nights while meandering the great floods, yours need to hold tight until your child reaches their post-teen years. That's what I call running a tight ship.

While taking all of this into consideration, your ODD child is not the only component your life consists of and you do have other priorities, many that have been discussed in earlier chapters. Slipping up is going to happen. Making mistakes is inevitable. If your child becomes aware of this, they are going to use it as a trigger to react and misbehave because, even though they've been systematically weaned off the toxic behavior through your positive and consistent approach, they still have a psychiatric disorder, and they are neurologically wired to act that way. Don't let it get to you. Nip it in the bud by going on exactly the way you did before it happened. People make mistakes, but unfortunately, your child is not in a position to understand that yet.

Calm Down Your ODD Child

In most cases, when an ODD child or teen is on the verge of doing something aggressive or losing it completely, we counter this negative behavior with a negative word like "no" or "don't" or even a phrase like "stop that." At this point, the child is so sensitive to their own emotional instability that countering their behavior with a word like 'no' can send them over the edge. For most of us, the word no is negative, yes, but if someone tells us 'no,' we'll likely comply and not be triggered by its negative nature. Well, not an ODD child or teen. As with many scenarios we've discussed in this book, parents try their best to prevent and help, but their methods just seem to fuel the flames exactly because of these small details we overlook. I don't think anyone will deny that ODD resembles rebellious behavior, only it is much more complicated. And, what happens if you say no, don't, or "stop" to a rebellious individual? You can expect the opposite reaction.

Here's a technique that's going to make you giggle. Hopefully, your child will also giggle because that's the point! Try using a codeword instead of words that communicate negative reinforcement like 'no' and the other ones we discussed earlier. You can either choose a word without discussing it with your child, or you can choose a word together so your child can use the word as well to warn you when they're about to have an episode. Imagine noticing that your child is blowing up and getting red in the face because they have to take out the trash and you just look at them and say 'swigglypoo' instead of using negative language. Their jaws just might drop to the floor. This can be your codeword for all words that indicate negative reinforcement. When you see that mouth opening in protest… "remember dear, swigglypoo." Or, "But mom…" "I said, SWIG-GLY-POOOOOO." They'll know what it means in no time.

Alternatively, you and your ODD child or teen can work together by choosing a codeword, and your child can let you know when they are feeling an aggressive episode coming. This will require a discussion with your child, which can also be a positive experience for them. You can empower your child by allowing them to choose the word and then you can talk about what should happen if they give you the codeword. For example, should you go for a quick walk around the block? Or, maybe you should go and shoot some hoops. I would just put on some loud music and start dancing like a crazy person to make my child laugh. Soon enough, they'll be dancing with you.

Work With your Child's Teachers and School

If your child is not being homeschooled by yours truly or your partner, you need to discuss your child's condition with their teacher or teachers, and any other individuals who may need to be aware of the possible complications it can cause. This is because, when it comes to learning, an ODD child is most often a special needs child, especially if they have co-occurring conditions that involve ADHD, or language learning or cognition issues. For example, whether your child is attending school online or going to school, you can ask the teacher to remove any distracting items in the background of the online classroom like multicolored posters. Alternatively, if your child will be sitting in an actual classroom, you can ask the teacher to seat them in the front, where they won't be able to see so much movement from the students behind them.

Another example of something small that can make a big difference in an ODD child's behavior is making class activities very structured, and it will work extremely well if the teacher can provide a large planner on the wall in a physical classroom where all the students can see it or a digital one the teacher and your child has access to in an online setting, which indicates when they are going to do what during class. This structural addition is very important and can spare you a lot of arguments and conflict in the classroom setting.

It may be hard to discuss all these requirements with your child's teacher, but they may not have dealt with an ODD child before, and while it may seem to them that you want to change their teaching style, most of the information you provide them is to make their day as conflict-free as possible. It's crucial for them to understand this because, if they don't and they find your approach a bit overbearing, they may consider ignoring your advice altogether, which they will regret for a long time. I decided to mention this now because the next aspect you may want to discuss with a teacher is how they communicate with the students. Instead of providing information and expecting the students to accept it for what it is, it is much more prudent to follow an approach where you engage them in the discussion, especially if there's an opinionated ODD student present. By following this approach, the teacher gives the ODD child an opportunity for a healthy release, which lessens the chance of a build up and subsequent explosion later.

The next suggestion is for the teacher to include a program or lessons about emotional regulation that actively focuses on teaching children how to handle powerful emotions like anger and frustration. This can be easily organized if your child is attending school online; however, if that is not the case, you may have to organize a meeting with the school staff. You can also enquire about bullying and well-being programs that teach children how to be resilient when they have to face tough situations like these.

Finally, it is very important for the teacher or teachers to understand the required balance between rewards versus punishment. It's pointless if you, as the parent, have a great and healthy system going at home, but your child's teachers at school do not focus on rewarding your child at all because they are only focusing on their bad behavior. It's like building up your child and sending them to school just to be broken down again. Always make sure that, whether your child attends school in an online setting or physical setting, that the teacher has a profound understanding of how important positive reinforcement is for the well-being of your child (raisingchildren.net.au, 2020).

Empower the Siblings

If your ODD child or teen has siblings, they are probably dealing with the same stress and aggression you are. Having an ODD child and other children is going to require you to not only divide your focus but also turn each eye into a super-powered laser beam, at least at the beginning when a system has not been established yet and your household is relatively chaotic.

Why it's Difficult

The nature of the relationships between ODD children and teens and their siblings resemble a constant power struggle because your ODD child is on a constant mission to control everything. Sharing, considering another's wants and needs, and playing nice are not ideas that likely exist in their minds, and these concepts will have to be planted and cultivated with care and patience. Meanwhile, you have to look after the well-being of your other children, and it is important for them to understand the situation without retaliating in a confrontational situation by bullying your ODD child due to their condition.

Siblings may react in ways like these because of the high levels of stress and frustration they have to deal with. As parents, we can all understand that this is not a healthy environment for them, and it can cause feelings of resentment if they feel that their ODD sibling gets away with misbehavior without being properly punished. They may feel neglected and become rebellious against how the household is being run because of the hurt and anger they are experiencing. A common strategy parents use when children fight is to let them sort out their issues or differences on their own. However, this is not a prudent strategy when one of the siblings has ODD. Because they take conflict and aggressive behavior to a completely new level and have no interest in sorting out the issue, your intervention is crucial.

Teach Them to Look for Signs

One strategy you can teach your affected siblings is to identify the warning signs and to shut down the communication completely and leave their ODD sibling alone. For example, you can ask your child, "have you noticed what your brother does before he throws a tantrum?" Your child may say, "Yes, he balls his fists and he gets red in the face." If you can see that your child has identified these warning signs, tell them to just turn around and walk away. Tell them, "I know it's hard because your brother's anger frustrates you. But if you just turn around and walk away, he has nobody to fight with." Avoid saying something like, "If you turn around and walk away, you'll be the better person." This will give your child the wrong idea, and the way you want to show your children that they are also important is not to use language that suggests you favoring them over your ODD child or teen.

Empower Them with Choices

Another important message your children need to hear from you is that it's okay for them to set boundaries and to recognize and respect the boundaries of other family members. They can claim their own emotional and physical space, and they can inform another family member if they've entered that space without their approval. Your children need to hear this from you as their parent because their ODD sibling is only aware of their own boundaries and not anyone else's. This is a way to empower your children by telling them that they also have a rightful place in the household, but they still need to deal with an invasion of space or a crossing of boundaries in a non-confrontational way. This should not be a reason for them to fight with their ODD sibling.

Redress

The implementation of fair restitution by you will mean a lot to your affected siblings. In a household with an ODD child, making fairness a priority will help the siblings to feel worthy, experience fewer feelings of resentment, and give them a feeling of belonging. This implementation of redress is, of course, meant to go both ways, and your children should understand that. So, if one of your siblings is in the wrong, restitution will be applied the same way it would have if the culprit was their ODD sibling. This should be done in an almost stoic fashion, where emotions do not rule the actions taken in such a situation, but rather the actions themselves. For example, the restitution or redress should not be done with an air of "oh, it's you this time, is it?" Turn your face into a blank slate that is unreadable so your children can shift their focus to your actions. If you do this for the first few times, there may be some bombs exploding in your house. Just keep that consistency going. You show your child that you love them, so no guilty feelings allowed!

Praise Initiative

When you start implementing new rules in your household, chances are you are going to experience a lot of resistance and possibly aggression. However, there is also a chance that your children may develop the ability to solve problems on their own that could've ended up in conflict situations, especially if you expose them to a positive and proactive environment at home. These attempts and successes should be celebrated as they are an indication of growth, especially if they involve communication between your ODD child or teen and a sibling.

Praise their efforts and always help them to understand how it contributes to your family goal of being a cohesive and loving unit (Abraham & Studaker, 2020).

Conclusion

As I write the final part of this book, I wonder where each reader will be in their journey with their ODD child or teen. The beginning is terribly confusing, especially if you didn't know much about the existence of Oppositional Defiant Disorder before the diagnosis. Then, the post-diagnosis phase can be just as confusing because you are not sure which treatment is best for your child, and treatment without solid reinforcement and consistency at home may not be as successful as you'd hoped. The one thing that a parent needs to understand when they are dealing with a child or teen that has ODD is that their ODD children should always be subject to the same rules that have the same consequences. No leeway. It is only this stronghold of consistency that initiates the process of mellowing them down and improving the atmosphere at home.

This guide provides information, advice, and suggestions from a multitude of perspectives that are truly aimed at a holistic approach for improving you and your family's life while living with an ODD child or teen. One thing you may have noticed is that, even though each chapter discusses different topics, it is clearly suggested that all the information in this guide should be used together to tame the stormy waters of Oppositional Defiant Disorder. Each part fits into the next, and with one part missing, there's going to be a gap or a loophole that will cause you and your family to have to start all over again. And, that's what makes dealing with an ODD child and teen such a challenge. Being human and making mistakes or being inconsistent is simply not acceptable to these children. It draws out that aggression and defiance that causes the whole family anxiety. If you accidentally give a sibling a larger piece of candy, there's going to be ruckus all afternoon. If you have the strength to take a step back and look at how your child is acting, you may just have to swallow a laugh. So, here's what you're going to do moving forward:

Keep the discussion about ODD as a source of reference, as well as all the treatment types and what they entail. Keep in mind that you still need a doctor for a diagnosis.

Focus on your 3 P's as they are your golden treasure chest. If you are riddled with anxiety and depression, push yourself to practice self-care as you now know how important looking after yourself is for your kids.

Don't feel guilty about anything. This is a positive turning point. Get your family together, find your goal and do everything you do in life to honor that goal. Be positive with your children and empower them. Remember how your ODD child's mind works, and consider how social referencing impacts your little one. Most importantly, have as much patience as you can possibly muster, and then some. While it may be difficult, remind yourself, over and over, of the importance of what you're doing and the love that empowers your every word and action. You can do this. Additionally, don't forget to be in touch with the school or teachers. They need to know, so don't be shy to tell them what your child needs to succeed academically. They should be prepared and willing

This is your time to take control. This is your time to shine. Show your children how much you love them, and show your family how important they are to you. Remember, Positivity, Proactivity, and Patience, with a large dash of Consistency!

About The Author

Kathleen is an award-winning writer and mother to a child who has been diagnosed with Oppositional Defiant Disorder at an early age. After experiencing difficulties coping as a parent, Kathleen started closely observing the behaviors of her own child and combined these observations with in-depth research to ultimately improve the health and well-being of her child. Kathleen subsequently created a multifaceted guide aimed at helping other parents and guardians deal with children diagnosed with Oppositional Defiant Disorder and its symptoms. Kathleen has always had a passion for psychology and how its theories are interconnected to specific neurological functions within the human brain. It was upon graduating college with honors that Kathleen went on to pursue her love of writing, and her journey, inspired by motherhood, is to help other parents overcome any issues or barriers they may face with raising a child or teenager with Oppositional Defiant Disorder.

References

A Conscious Rethink. (2019, July 22). *8 ways to be more proactive in life (+ examples).* A Conscious Rethink. https://www.aconsciousrethink.com/11064/be-proactive/

Abraham, K., & Studaker, M. (2020). *Sibling fighting: 5 ways to teach your kids to work it out.* Empowering Parents. https://www.empoweringparents.com/article/odd-child-and-sibling-fighting/

Achwal, A. (2020, April 24). *Impact of social referencing on child's development.* Parenting.Firstcry.Com. https://parenting.firstcry.com/articles/role-of-social-referencing-in-childs-overall-development/

Additude. (2016, November 28). *6 essential, natural supplements for ADHD.* ADDitude. https://www.additudemag.com/slideshows/adhd-supplements-fish-oil-zinc-iron/#:~:text=What%20Is%20Zinc%20Good%20For

ADHD Editorial Board. (2018, April 27). *8 discipline rules: Oppositional defiant disorder strategies.* ADDitude. https://www.additudemag.com/oppositional-defiant-disorder-discipline-rules-video/

Balance, B. (2019). *3 tips for working with oppositional defiance in teens.* Brainbalancecenters.Com. https://blog.brainbalancecenters.com/2017/01/tips-working-oppositional-defiance-teens

Benjamin, A. E. (2020). *The importance of family teamwork - metrofamily magazine.* Www.Metrofamilymagazine.Com. https://www.metrofamilymagazine.com/the-importance-of-family-teamwork/

Brookshire, B. (2016, August 5). *Hormone affects how teens' brains control emotions.* Science News for Students. https://www.sciencenewsforstudents.org/article/hormone-affects-how-teens-brains-control-emotions

CHADD. (2018). *The benefits of sports on ADHD can be golden - CHADD.* CHADD. https://chadd.org/adhd-weekly/the-benefits-of-sports-on-adhd-can-be-golden/

Cherry, K. (2012, March 5). *Benefits of positive thinking for body and mind.* Verywell Mind; Verywellmind. https://www.verywellmind.com/benefits-of-positive-thinking-2794767

Child Mind Institute. (2020a). *Intellectual development disorder basics.* Child Mind Institute. https://childmind.org/guide/intellectual-development-disorder/

Child Mind Institute. (2020b). *Language disorder basics.* Child Mind Institute. https://childmind.org/guide/language-disorder/

Coryell, W. (2020, March). *Depressive disorders - psychiatric disorders.* MSD Manual Professional Edition. https://www.msdmanuals.com/professional/psychiatric-disorders/mood-disorders/depressive-disorders

Delancy, A. (2015, July 4). *The importance of teamwork in families.* The Behaviourist Guy. https://stepstoexcellence.wordpress.com/2015/07/04/the-importance-of-teamwork-in-families/

Demko, S. (2018, September 14). *Omega-3 fatty acids may help ease anxiety symptoms.* Www.Healio.Com. https://www.healio.com/news/psychiatry/20180914/omega3-fatty-acids-may-help-ease-anxiety-symptoms#:~:text=0.08%2D0.67).-

Ekeland, E., Jamtvedt, G., Heian, F., & Hagen, K. B. (2006). Exercise for oppositional defiant disorder and conduct disorder in children and adolescents. *Cochrane Database of Systematic Reviews.* https://doi.org/10.1002/14651858.cd005651

Elia, J. (2019, March). *Overview of Mental Health Disorders in Children - Children's Health Issues.* MSD Manual Consumer Version. https://www.msdmanuals.com/en-kr/home/children-s-health-issues/mental-health-disorders-in-children-and-adolescents/overview-of-mental-health-disorders-in-children

Ferguson, S. (2019, March 20). *Magnesium for anxiety: How you can fight anxiety and feel better.* Healthline. https://www.healthline.com/health/magnesium-anxiety#which-magnesium

Harvard Health Blog. (2020). *The adolescent brain: Beyond raging hormones.* Harvard Health. https://www.health.harvard.edu/mind-and-mood/the-adolescent-brain-beyond-raging-hormones#:~:text=Hormonal%20changes%20are%20at%20work

Health Agenda. (2017, October). *Why are whole foods good for you? | HCF.* Www.Hcf.Com.Au. https://www.hcf.com.au/health-agenda/food-diet/nutrition/what-are-wholefoods#:~:text=The%20whole%20food%20advantage&text=The%20benefits%20of%20a%20whole

Jeanie Lerche Davis. (2003, February 2). *What are anxiety disorders?* WebMD; WebMD. https://www.webmd.com/anxiety-panic/guide/anxiety-disorders#1

Kruger, P. (2005, October 5). *Staying lovers while raising kids.* Parents; Parents. https://www.parents.com/parenting/relationships/staying-close/staying-lovers-while-raising-kids/

Mauro, T. (2020, May 5). *Resources for parents of kids with oppositional defiant disorder.* Verywell Mind. https://www.verywellmind.com/before-you-look-for-information-on-odd-3106614

Mayo Clinic. (2018). *Oppositional defiant disorder ODD*. Mayoclinic.Org. https://www.mayoclinic.org/diseases-conditions/oppositional-defiant-disorder/symptoms-causes/syc-20375831

Mayo Clinic. (2020). *Intermittent explosive disorder - symptoms and causes*. Mayo Clinic. https://www.mayoclinic.org/diseases-conditions/intermittent-explosive-disorder/symptoms-causes/syc-20373921

Mayo Clinic Staff. (2020). *Vitamin E*. Mayo Clinic. https://www.mayoclinic.org/drugs-supplements-vitamin-e/art-20364144#:~:text=Vitamin%20E%20also%20has%20antioxidant

Morin, A. (2019). *The secret to getting your child to behave is easier than you think*. Verywell Family. https://www.verywellfamily.com/how-to-use-praise-to-promote-good-behavior-1094892

Morin, A. (2020a, January 31). *15 self-care strategies for busy parents* (C. Sneider, Ed.). Verywell Family. https://www.verywellfamily.com/self-care-for-parents-4178010

Morin, A. (2020b, September 30). *Strategies for parenting a child with oppositional defiant disorder*. Verywell Family. https://www.verywellfamily.com/oppositional-defiant-disorder-discipline-1094924

National Scientific Council on the Developing Child. (2004). *Children's emotional development is built into the architecture of their brains: Working paper no. 2*. Developingchild.Net; Harvard University. http://www.developingchild.net

PowerofPositivity. (2014, October 30). *10 ways positive thinking improves your health | power of positivity*. Power of Positivity: Positive Thinking & Attitude. https://www.powerofpositivity.com/10-ways-positive-thinking-improves-health/

PROactive Parenting. (2020). *What's proactive parenting? Mindful effective parenting w/o yelling*. Proactive Parenting.

https://proactiveparenting.net/about-proactive-parenting/#:~:text=Proactive%20Parenting%20is%20all%20about

raisingchildren.net.au. (2020). *Oppositional defiant disorder (ODD): children 5-12 years.* Raising Children Network. https://raisingchildren.net.au/guides/a-z-health-reference/odd

Rowden, D. (2020). *How to be a more patient parent | tips on parenting patience.* Empowering Parents. https://www.empoweringparents.com/article/4-steps-to-more-patience-as-a-parent/

Shattuck, L. (2018, September 5). *8 tips for how to have a healthy relationship (even with kids).* Meetfabric.Com. https://meetfabric.com/blog/how-to-have-a-healthy-relationship-married-with-kids

Stanford Children's Health. (2019). *Organized sports for kids.* Stanfordchildrens.Org. https://www.stanfordchildrens.org/en/topic/default?id=organized-sports-for-kids-1-4556

Steinkraus, A. (2015, August 15). *The power of patience.* Cornell Cooperative Extension. http://ccetompkins.org/family/parent-pages/just-for-parents/the-power-of-patience#:~:text=The%20power%20of%20patience%20helps

Tottenham, N. (2017, July 18). *The brain's emotional development.* Dana Foundation. https://dana.org/article/the-brains-emotional-development/

Valley Behavioral Health System. (2017). *Signs, symptoms & effects of ODD | valley behavioral health.* Www.Valleybehavioral.Com. https://www.valleybehavioral.com/disorders/odd/signs-symptoms-causes/#:~:text=Oppositional%20defiant%20disorder%20(ODD)%20is

Welcome Cure. (2020). *Oppositional defiant disorder (ODD) Homeopathic Treatment.* Www.Welcomecure.Com. https://www.welcomecure.com/diseases/oppositional-defiant-disorder-odd/homeopathic-treatment

CPSIA information can be obtained
at www.ICGtesting.com
Printed in the USA
BVHW092251301120
594477BV00010B/1708

9 781736 004616